THE
MAVERICK
AND
HIS MOVES

THE
MAVERICK
AND
HIS MOVES

MUKESH YADAV

PARTRIDGE

ISBN: Softcover   978-1-4828-7534-8
             eBook   978-1-4828-7533-1

Print information available on the last page.

To order additional copies of this book, contact
Partridge India
000 800 10062 62
orders.india@partridgepublishing.com

www.partridgepublishing.com/india

1

An Entertainer

Shahrukh Khan- a very well established name in India. He is a man who everywhere represents India, and particularly modern India. He represents the intelligence, knowledgeable and a very well informed part of India. He is an actor who defines the spirit of Bollywood-the Hindi Language Film industry based in Mumbai. He is a symbol of Indian national Pride. He has inspired many aspiring Indians with his energy, sheer charm, intelligence and love for everyone. With a huge fan base around the world, he is one of the most influential Indian on the global stage.

Born in New Delhi in 1965, Shahrukh Khan was a keen scholar, excelling in studies and sports. Determined to pursue a career in theatre, he trained at the National school of drama. He has been active in Hindi films since 1992. Before this, he appeared in several television series. He made his debut on television in 1989 in a very successful series *fauji* in which he portrayed an Army cadet. He was much applauded for his work. He got film offers and became a movie star. He made his film debut in the Hindi movie "*Deewana* (1992)" and won the prestigious filmfare award for best debut actor-male. Through his films, he gave certain ideas of love and happiness. After making his Bollywood debut with this box-office hit film, he became synonymous for portraying villainous roles. His rise to prominence continues after starring in series of romantic dramas, establishing him as an icon of romance in India and winning widespread adulation from audiences. Throughout his career, he has broken numerous box-office records. His illustrious filmy career has delivered some of the most memorable and award winning commercial hits of Hindi Cinema.

"King Khan" as he is known among his fans is a self-made man with a string of achievements attached to his name. He lost his parents when he was young. He came to Mumbai with very small amount of money and a Videocon television that his mother gave him before she died. He feels very happy and proud of the fact that he is one of the most well-known name in the world but he tries to act very humble about that. He had a very humble beginning and he never forgotten that in his choice of films that he makes and characters that he portrays. Despite of all his success, he maintains his humility. He likes to tell everyone that he is the humble servant of the image that he has created. He believes that the best way to thank God is by being humble. It is the best way of thanking life for giving an existence. It is the key word, which distinguishes him from the others.

From the time, he first began working as an actor in television; he has been a constant presence for Indian audiences. His journey to become a superstar is full of will, determination and sheer belief in oneself. He has been Bollywood's biggest newsworthy item. His arrival and rise in the Indian film Industry has been a story of unprecedented Success. His phenomenal rise to success and stardom has inspired an entire generation of India. The dimensions of his stardom are mind-blowing. The standard of his Success is very large.

From humble beginning in Delhi to super-stardom and unimaginable success, Shahrukh Khan is an example of how sometimes the most courageous dreams come true. He has redefined what success in the Indian Entertainment Industry means. He rules over the Hindi cinema along with the heart of legion of fans all around the world. His urban classy style found several admirers in India as well as abroad. The audience loves his boy next-door charm. The women loves his dimples and men loves his distinctive sense of style and charisma. He makes film that involves certain kinds of emotions that appeal to every sensibility. He tries to create cinema or entertainment at the level that he knows best. His catchy dialogues are spread all over the world and the main reason he has earned a particular place in the hearts of millions of people is that he has created a style of his own. New and young directors like to work with him so that they can push the boundaries not only in terms of commerce but also in terms of number of people who come and watch the film. He makes movies with lots of goodness and passion. There are so many expectations on him from the director, producer, distributor and audience side but he never falls short of that expectation.

Shahrukh Khan is an International figure. He is one of the most acclaimed actors in India and overseas. His contribution to Hindi Cinema has made him a global figure. His talent and generosity arouses the enthusiasm of vast audience across the world. He has a kind of global acceptance which a very few Indians have seen in their lifetime. By many measures, he is one of world's biggest movie star. In 2008, Newsweek, a US based magazine, recognized him among the 50 most powerful people in the world. In 2011, the Los Angeles times described him as "Perhaps the world's biggest movie-star." His star appeal has spread around the globe. He joins the League of biggest stars of the Indian film Industry and Western cinema when it comes to popularity. His films appeal and unite the audiences, which are normally odd to each other. He makes movies not just for India but for overseas market as well. The popularity of Shahrukh Khan in abroad can be measured from the fact that his movies witness significant opening in international market. He has everything that makes him one of the most successful celebrities of the world.

He represents the Indian Film Industry in a big way. With a huge spread of Indian community outside India, his movies are making lasting impression on them. He has carved out an audience of his own across the world. His success transcends all boundaries and nationalities. His success and individuality reflects an amalgam of urban, secular and western identity. He is a humble servant of Indian Cinema who has taken it to the shores, which have not understood, seen or experienced Indian Cinema. For Indian living abroad, Bollywood is a religion and Shahrukh Khan is a god. People from sub-continent are the ones responsible for his super stardom because his films done very well there. His films personify everything that is good about India. The movies focus on family. They have a strong base that many western films do not have. That is something missing from Hollywood films. Roles, which Shahrukh Khan plays, touch everyone abroad in that way. In his career, the films that he has done are highly responsible. All these films have a huge Indian values attached to them and they are presented in a way, which appeals to every section of the society. They are mix of Indian culture and family values. Khan's films speak that language and somewhere the western audience understands that language. They understand the family values, music, dance and the colors that Indian cinema has. Due to this, he appeals to the International audience.

As an actor or a star, he has a great sustaining power. He has created a space in the Indian Film Industry. He is a book by himself in which there are various stories and each story is so interesting and entertaining. People of all segments love him. Therefore, to describe Shahrukh Khan as a legend would be no exaggeration.

Shahrukh Khan is a versatile actor. He has explored different possible zones in his extraordinary life. Apart from cinema work, he has climbed several peaks. He is an actor, an entrepreneur, a television personality, a brand endorser, an anchor, a motivational speaker, a producer, a philanthropist and sometimes all at once. He has appeared in several Hindi films in genres like romance, action, superhero and comedy. He owns Red Chillies Entertainment, a production and distribution company. As a producer, he has the creative freedom to make the films that he wants to make. He is the co-owner of IPL winning team Kolkata Knight Riders and owns shares in Kidzania Mumbai- the Indian franchise of the indoor edutainment theme park. In addition, he participates in several award shows as a host or stage performer. That is why, he is more than just a movie star in India.

Emergence of an Entertainer

Shahrukh Khan's core competence is acting and that is what he enjoys the most. He has been able to make acting a successful profession. People have made him a big actor because of his on-screen presence and the number of awards that he gets but he is inherently an entertainer. Over the years, he has evolved as an entertainer, who won the hearts of millions of people through his extensive body of work and abandon charisma. He stands for Entertainment. He wants people to be entertained. He does everything wholeheartedly and with passion, which is quite fascinating to the audience. For him the most important part of being an actor is to entertain people and that entertainment can be sad, musical, bright, colorful and, at the same time, can be silly also. He services the nation in that way. That is how he likes to describe himself. He works very hard to retain the position of entertainment that he has. He believes that as an employee of Indian Cinema, it is his duty to please the audience more than they expect from him. "It's not only a challenge, it's my duty to please you more than you expect me to please you," he said.

Entertainment is the intrinsic quality of actor Shahrukh Khan. He has earned a peak position in the entertainment field. Every venture of Shahrukh Khan has come from the desire to entertain people. He tries to bring new things in every movie. The core that he wanted when he started his career is same that he wants today. He wants to entertain people. He wants them to smile. That has not changed. The methods might have changed but the bottom-line and result is to entertain people with lot of honesty and purity. He is an artist who can entertain people in any medium. He can entertain on films, TV, radio and many other platforms. He enjoys every platform. He is an example of an entertainer by all standards. He entertains people in different ways possible and takes the viewer to a world, which provides them a medium of escape from the painful realities of life.

The greatest desire of Shahrukh Khan's life is to bring smiles to people's faces. He loves the fact that on Fridays he makes people smile. He feels extremely wonderful being able to make people laugh. He likes to make people happy than get happier. Whether he is happy or sad, he can spread his arms in middle of thousand persons and make them smile. This is the job that he is meant to do.

As an entertainer, he has contributed a lot to the all-round well-being of the society. He dedicated his life to entertain people in different ways possible and always moves ahead to expand his entertainment empire. From the beginning, he left an impression on everyone. He is able to fulfill the desires of every Indian cinegoer. It is to his credit that he knows the pulse of any age. He charms people across ages, gender and geographical boundaries.

Despite his success in the Indian film Industry, Shahrukh Khan has no pretension about just being an entertainer. He considers himself a monkey that dances on the road and pleases everyone. That is the only importance that he attaches to himself. Many a time, he says 'I am a *Nautanki* guy,' who is meant to entertain people. He says this with great pride and huge amount of respect that he has for entertainment.

By virtue of being an actor, he has a vast experience of Life, humanity and people. He catches on very fast what is happening. When he comes in a room or gets into an interactive session with people, he feels the love. Even if the numbers of people in a room are very less, he keeps laughing, chatting and engaging with them. He likes to please them and make them happy. "Even if everybody sitting in the dark and a strange and a scary thing which I can tell you, I observe and I notice everyone. I know how they breathe how they talk what they walk like their smile means what. It is an analysis, which I do in about 5 seconds. It's instinctive." He mentioned by adding that "I can give a hug to a person who doesn't even know me but I know he or she is right now very sad. This hug will change her life for .01 seconds. She just need it or he just need it and I hope I can do that to everyone who sees me."

Shahrukh Khan has a very deep thinking about making a film. He has worked in films, which required in-depth thinking and ideas but, before believing in all, he believes in entertainment. He has mentioned on several forums that he always work towards making or being part of a Cinema that entertains all and meant for all. He has never made claims to be somebody who does experiments with his roles and gives audience a great performance. The bottom line of the films in which he acted is entertainment, nothing else at all. He gives more importance to a film that appeal to the audience in terms of entertainment. He tries to do films which most of the people like to see. The process of trying to make people happy and smile is more important than the result of the film. He does not want any other baggage attached to it. His job is to bring smile on the faces of people. This is the greatest gift that god has given him that he is able to bring smile on the faces of people when they see him. He cannot led his beliefs to bore the audience. They should enjoy the story and remain happy for 3 hours in the dark room.

He does not make films to give any kind of message to the audience or to change their life. Essentially, he makes films just to tell a story. He just makes them to make the audience happy and entertained. He believes that the films that he does are for entertainment. Within it, if they hide a little message of the things that he believes, it is nice but they should not overtake the entertainment. He has always said that messages are for post offices. Films are for entertainment. They have a role in discussing and examining social issues but if they make it a prime concern then they do not remain films. They do not remain entertainment.

Mechanisms of Acting

Shahrukh Khan is a prepared actor. He prepares things before doing that. He does lot of things with techniques. He has mannerisms. He meets so many people. He loves to talk to them and gets to know them. Thus, when he gets a role, he just takes instances from life and use it. He tries to keep it simple and real. Sometimes people say it is over the top. It is too simplistic but it reaches out to everyone. It touches everybody's heart and people identify with it.

He has a completely different way of doing a character. In his career, he has made diverse range of films. He has done variety of roles but he does not follow a set pattern. He has a taste and choice in films that he wants to do. He feels like doing different things in different state of mind and space. He gets bored by doing same thing. He has played roles from various films genres: Romantic, Comedies, Action, Thriller, Dramas and Superheroes films. As a theatre actor, he always wanted to play different characters in the parameters of commercial cinema. He feels extremely important to experience different worlds of cinema that any director, producer or writer creates. Therefore, he always tries to run away from an image before it typecast him. He likes to play character roles or protagonist in his films. As long as he can, he hopes his performances and star value is such that he plays protagonist in as many films as he can. However, he does not make any concerted effort to design films that suits him. People gave too much importance to how he thinks and do a film. He likes to do what he feels like doing. After years of experience, he still does not have the understanding whether the film is going to work or not. He acts in a film because it feels nice at that point of time. He does not make a conscious decision to choose a film. He just do films that excites him. He has something, which connects with the people that cannot be describable and that may not work for many others.

Shahrukh Khan has no enigma around acting. He does not go deeply into acting. He just enjoys himself and let the others enjoy themselves. Critics, many a times, write about his mannerisms of acting. They talk about under-playing and over-playing of acting. However, he does not believe in any method of acting. He likes to perform with the prime objective of providing entertainment to the audience. "There is nothing like right way to do a scene and a wrong way to do a scene. There is just a way to do a scene. Your way, my way, any way could be right," he observed. His work ethics tells him that whatever role is given, he should try to make it his dream role rather than sitting down and waiting for a dream role. Thus, he tries to make it as good as possible and perhaps creates something, which is new and interesting.

Acting is very spiritual to him. It combines all sorts of soulful, religious spiritual things that people do. He does not consider himself as a good actor. He truly believes that there is nothing like a good actor because every time the products, lines and characters are new, then how one can makes a permanent statement that this person is a good actor. It always has to be like did he play this well? Did he play that well?

Many people seems to know that Acting is about wearing masks, faces and expressions. However, the actor has a belief that Acting is about taking off the masks, letting people see and reveal to them that you are exactly the same person as they are. Even the talent that he has as an actor is about taking off all the masks and just letting everyone see that you enjoy the same thing as they do. He believes in the saying that "Acting is not about letting people come into the auditorium and see who you are, but holding up a mirror and showing who they are." Actors are not special just because they happened to come on a big screen and look bigger. All of us are the same. He finds wrong when actors walks on the stage with an aura around themselves. The actor believes that nobody pays money just to see people in any profession. As soon as the audience has paid money to come into the hall, they are already giving you respect. They have already accepted that you are a nice person or a big person. There is an immense amount of responsibility that people expect from him. There is an immense amount of entertainment that they want from him. He never tries to impress them with his aura. He tries to keep it simple. With this kind of attitude, the relation between the artist and the audience become much better.

Shahrukh Khan is an example of somebody who knew how to stretch his boundaries and achieve what he had to achieve. He has achieved heights that one can dream. He was not born into a world of fame and glory. He is an outsider. When he came to Mumbai, he had no connection with the Indian film Industry. He did not have a record of accomplishment. He was not aware of the film culture. Because of that, he could worked with lot of freedom. He had nothing to lose and had the courage to beat the conventional image of a hero. He deliberately challenged the conventional roles because he did not want to do the regular things. Therefore, very quickly, he changed the rule of the game and take up the role of a villain in some of his initial films like *Baazigar* (1993), *Darr* (1993) and *Anjaam* (1994). He gained popularity by playing such negative roles. He played those characters with heart. He likes the idea of evil being mesmerizing. There is something inside him, which wants to come out and play that is evil. It is something that he believed he could do it and worked towards it. These films, somewhere, gave him unpredictability as an actor for a period of years. Shahrukh Khan ruled the 1990s with films like *Dilwale Dulhania Le jayenge* (1996) and *Kuch Kuch hota hai* (1998). These films created a nationwide hysteria and soon he became the Indian heartthrob. While the critics said that, he was type casted with *Raj* and *Rahul* but it did not seem to make a difference to his growing fan base. He kept delivering one hit after another, redefining himself with films like *Swades* (2004), *Chakde India* (2007) and *My name is Khan* (2010), which were different from his usual romantic roles.

As an actor, Shahrukh Khan does not find things challenging. He has been working for too long to call a film or role challenging. He is a believer of the fact that if you start making big thing out of it, it would not be as enjoyable and interesting for people to watch. He works very hard for every film that he does. He does not show it but he personally dislikes actors discussing how they worked on a role unless they are discussing with their co-actors or directors. He finds it extremely boring to explain the process of acting and challenges that has gone to do a role. He writes his roles. He makes notes of his script. He stands in front of mirror and practices it.

Every generation falls in love with Shahrukh Khan. There is a purity and innocence in his films. The films were not designed for people of any generation. The characters were created like this. In his career, he has made films where he was trying to be different. He tried to create characters in movies like *Swades* (2004), *Chakde India* (2007) and *My name is Khan* (2010) because he started enjoying that and people appreciated this. They loved him in those films more than they loved him in regular commercial films. He is also very fortunate that he has a few characters by which people recognize him like Baadshah, Baazigar, Rahul or Raj. He finds it great to known by the names of the characters of his films. He thinks the biggest compliment an actor can get is to be called by the name of his character when the film is released. He wants to create a few characters like these and he is not worried about such comparisons. He wants to work hard and create characters by which people will know him. He is always asked which is your best character and he says- the next one. The previous one is over. Every time he finishes a film, he still believes he can make a better film.

Shahrukh Khan thinks it is not the actor's job to explain how much he is attached to a character and how he creates it. He has never done it. Therefore, it does not come across that Shahrukh Khan is a serious actor. He is highly intelligent and a serious actor. He develops a walk. He develops a voice. He loves the character that he creates. He just does not speak seriously about it. He is so self-deprecating and makes fun about the work that he does. What he does means a lot to him as an actor and takes away a huge part of his insides. "Genuinely I am giving a part of me to every character that I make so much so I have a fear that one morning I'll wake up and I'll have no parts to give to any more characters. That's god's honest truth," he mentioned. When it does not hit the target, it really saddens him. It means that a part of something that he has given his life has not been able to hold up to the excellence that he wanted. Therefore, whatever the films that he has done, there is a little part of him in it whether it is his soul, heart or mind. It is not just a film. He has left something down there. Each of his film belongs to him, not in ownership way but in an emotional way.

Shahrukh Khan has a lot of Energy. He enjoys serious acting with somber expressions but, at the same time, he enjoys working with commercial thinking filmmakers who can entertain many people. Even in a commercial movie, he likes to work in a character, which he can pull off as an actor. He enjoys that most. The films, which are dark and morbid, are not what he likes.

Live stage shows

Shahrukh Khan did many theatres in the initial years of his acting and he believes that the closest he can come back to it is by doing concerts and tours. Throughout his career, Shahrukh Khan has been part of several live stage shows. In 2004, the Temptation concert tour was successfully performed across the United States and the Europe alongside other Indian stars. As an entertainer, he likes to perform at a huge scale in order to take the name of Indian films, and India forward. He manage to take time out from his busy schedule to appear in live stage shows through which he wants to retain the inherent quality of Bollywood, which is to entertain, interact and dance. Nobody can afford to miss his mesmerizing stage performances, which he does in various stage shows and award shows. He performs with lot of energy and happiness. He is known for his unrestrained enthusiasm, which enables him to perform beyond expectation. He is breathtaking to watch.

For big live stage shows or world tours, Shahrukh Khan prepares for around 30 days with dancers and choreographers. They write theme to it so that people do not get bored. There are enough entries and exit of stars so that at no given time, the stage is without a star, which the audience has come to see. Therefore, a lot of work goes in to it. It is a little more nerve wrecking. Technologically, many things can go wrong. If it goes wrong, it goes wrong. There is no chance of re-take. However, he tries to cover up mistakes on stage. The actor believes that sometimes covering up the mistake itself is an interesting take for the audience.

Live stage show is not equitable to anything else. The scream of audience gives a strange sense of feeling to realize what being a star is. He goes back from the stage shows knowing that a number of people love him.

Shahrukh Khan participates in live stage shows more for a reason of performance so that he can interact with the audience and give them an evening to remember in terms of pride and happiness. He performs in live shows and makes appearances so that he can meet and interact with at least some of the people who love him so much. His idea has never been to just sing and dance in a stage show, but to give people a chance to interact and feel happy for those two hours. Being a theatre actor, he likes live interaction with people whether it is through performance or hosting the show. He enjoys that a lot, because the feedback is immediate and it has an excitement, which is very different from filmmaking.

Shahrukh Khan believes that a film or any performance is made by the people who are watching it, not by the artists who are performing in it. The idea of a live stage show is to have a good time with the audience, not to give just value for money. It is not just about entries, doing dance and going away. It has to be interactive. It is the part of his stage performance to invite an audience member on stage and do some acting with them because he wants to make shows a little different. He is not a dancer or a singer. Finally, he is an actor. Thus, he believes that there should be some aspects of acting on a live stage show.

Most of the interaction with the audience is never prepared. He just invites people on stage and things happen. This is the part of live shows that he enjoys most. In a certain way, he knows what people like at that point of time. He has a strange connection with the audience where he can sense their feeling a little earlier and react to it faster. His mind works very fast. It is instinctive. His enactment with anything on stage is that spontaneous.

Art of Giving

Shahrukh Khan never afraid to enjoy his success. He worked extremely hard to earn his success. He worked through his way and created his life himself. He likes to live life in king size. However, he believes that living life king size does not mean taking, it means giving. All he wants to do is to be accepted, love and give. He has always said that a star has to be giving, not calculative and the only way he knows how to give back is to entertain people.

Entertainment is something, which is not selfish. It is for the others. He tries to give a part of him to entertain people. The whole thing in life is about supply and demand. People want so much from him so he gives them that much and what he gives is the creative part of him, which has to be very honest and clear.

He also believes that not everything is achievement oriented. Some things are about giving. In addition, he has been very gracious and giving because so much has been given to him in life. He has a feeling that he has been given a lot more than he deserves in terms of love, money, fame and happiness. He wants to return it back before it ends otherwise he would not be able to enjoy who he is at the end of his career. It is something that he owes to everyone. Therefore, he just keeps giving. He wants to give, happiness, entertainment and smiles to his various audience.

Work round the clock

Shahrukh Khan worships his work. After working for so many years, he still feels excited about doing work. He considers it the nicest thing that he can do. He truly exemplifies unremitting devotion to work. He wakes up every day in the morning and manages to do a number of things at a time. After years of fame and stardom, he has no complacency. He keeps working. He keeps going every day like this. He often claims to be workaholic. Nothing makes him happier than working with people or in front of a camera. As an artist, he has a lot of passion in trying to get things right. He does not take himself very seriously but as far as the seriousness of the work is concerned, he is immensely dedicated to work. It has become his defining Identity and religion of the actor. He has nicest things in life provided by God but nothing turns him on except working day and night. There is nothing that gives him more solace than work. He plugs a lot of emptiness in life by working continuously. He believes that there is nothing like an ultimate winner and there is nothing like an ultimate loser. One should just keep working because it is happy and fun to keep on doing new things. There are number of problems that he faces every day. In spite of this, he works round the clock and of course, he has returns beyond his expectations for that work. He deals with the problems and lives with it.

Shahrukh Khan is a self-deprecating actor. He is quite self-deprecating about his own work because he is a big believer of the fact that "Art is more important than the artist." He is very serious about his work but he does not take himself very seriously. He does not take his work that much serious that it overpowers him. Over the years, he has honed his art to a certain level and he can deliver what an audience wants. He takes that very seriously but he does not take himself very seriously. Therefore, he makes fun of himself and believes that as long as, he is able to perform, he wants his art to be remembered as something that entertain everyone more than him.

He is down to earth towards his work. He never brought in stardom, any personal problem or any personal belief in the greatness of work that he does. What is happening at the given point of time to him is the work. There is nothing beyond and before that. There is nothing like "I need to go now." Work never stops whether his back hurt or arm. He is a very high-end employee. He works for many people- Producers, TV Channels and films. "We work with the thought that it's work that will take us somewhere. While doing that, we don't realize when the work becomes our life. What we are, the reason we are, becomes our work," he mentioned.

He feels envious of people who relax and rest. He feels jealous of people who do not want to be successful. According to him, success will not come unless you are completely restless. A person cannot be restful and in peace if he wants to be successful. There is nothing like healthy living, good food and relaxation for a successful man.

People get stress because of work. He gets de-stress while working. He is almost restless when it comes to work. He always wants to be busy. If not, he gets bored. He does not relax at all. He loves his work and keeps doing it. Somewhere along the line, he sees people are not following him but he still keep running and keep doing what he wants to do. He believes in the fact that if you are a worker, if you like work, you should never complain about too much work because it is really worse when you do not have work. Thus, he cannot say no to work. The actor has seen himself struggling for work, getting work, being at the top, then not getting work and then coming back.

Over the years, Shahrukh Khan has lost the ideology of working professionally. He prefers working with people who treat him with gentleness. The person has to be easy, sweet and a good human being. More than the story, he likes the people who make film with him. He does a film for reasons like work, style, happiness, smiles, goodness, warmth and good hugs. If a person has too much self-importance in creating something, he does not work with him. If a filmmaker starts being mechanical with him about work, he does not work with him. He likes to work with a person who has the ability to accept the fact that they are taking a wrong shot.

Whenever he starts something, whether it is a film, ad or endorsement, he wants the process to be interesting and enjoyable because the result is not in his hand. He likes to be in a state of mind to do a certain kind of things. He believes that if the process is enjoyable, it is a possibility that People will enjoy it too. The last consumer will like it. He believes and thinks a lot about the Cinema that he does because it is the most important thing for him. It makes him feel that this is what he is made to do. Therefore, he makes movies with lot of love and care. Until he is very loving and caring about a movie, he does not get into it. There is no other reason for doing a movie. He does not do it for money. He does not do it for a director or a producer. He does a movie when he feels it is the right time to tell a story. It makes him feel good and when he feels good, he has noticed most of the time it makes everyone else, who is watching it, also feel good.

Like a Horse with blinkers

Actor Shahrukh Khan is very Competitive but he believes in positive competition. "I am amazingly competitive. I am very ambitious. I want to do what I do the best. Even if I am playing carom, I want to win it. If I am brushing my teeth, I do it, as there is no brushing tomorrow. Everything I do needs to be done with best of your capability. If you actually starts doing it with that kind of passion, believe me you never believe there is competition," he said while motivating young people in 2006.

The actor has a lot of respect for other people's work but he does not compete with others. He tries to compete with himself. Like a horse, he just keeps running his race with blinkers on. He does not look anyone else in the lane. He wants to beat his own failures. He wants to beat himself. What keeps him going is to make better movies. "I don't beat up anyone. I don't overtake anyone. I have said this often enough and I say it once more: I run my own race. You want to try, come on to the side lane, go for it, attempt it. Do what you wish to," the actor said.

After working so many years in the Indian film Industry, Shahrukh Khan has reached in a position where people feel that every new or young actor is competing with him. The actor works with many young actors who speaks the language or have the expression of their own generation. They come with different set of ideas and have mind of their own. He finds the experience of Working with them very interesting but he does not have any competitive spirit. It gives him a little odd thought when people compare him with them. He finds it a little unfair. However, he takes as an honor when he is compared with the old actors but he finds quite embarrassing when he is compared with the young actors. "I really believe I am sitting in a car of my own, with its own gears. As a matter of fact, that car is on a completely separate track from where all these youngsters wonderfully are running. So I don't need to be understanding and thinking about that. I just do my job. I have been given so much in terms of the work that I have done that it would be really extremely small of me to sit down and competing with newcomers," he said. He always tries to give his best at whatever he does. He feels that none of the younger actor should catch-up with him. They should be much bigger and better as themselves. They should try to take the Indian cinema forward with their talent and hard work. They should do the stuff, which helps Indian Cinema to grow.

Shahrukh Khan came to Mumbai to rule over the people who are existing in the world with all his goodness and simplicity. He is an individual or a self-made star and he likes it that way. Thus, as a self-made actor, he wants to create a category that does not exist before and will never exist after.

He spends a lot of time with the stars of older generation. When he meets them, he tries to learn the art of humility and dedication from them. He wants to take those points and imbibe them. He has that spirit but he does not have any competitive spirit with any of his co-actor.

Talking about competition, once he said, "Competition is normally with something that is bigger than you. Unfortunately, I wake up in the morning and I believe rightly or wrongly that my film is the biggest in the world and because my film is the biggest in the world and that's the belief I have, I don't think there can be anything bigger. So I don't have competition. I say this with honesty. I mean I am not trying to sound pompous or arrogant." He only compete with something that runs faster than him, jumps higher than him, laughs louder than him and screams better than him.

Going Hollywood

Over the years, there has been a constant comparison between Bollywood and Hollywood. Of course, Questions have usually be asked about Shahrukh Khan's interest in Hollywood but the idea of working in Hollywood movies does not excite him. He has confined himself to the Hindi cinema. He honestly believes that nobody from Hollywood is interested in him and he has nothing special to offer. He does not have anything special to offer which Hollywood does not have. He does not have an USP that can include him in a Hollywood film unless the film is called "brown Indian." However, he always tell that he is not willing to take up stereotypical role created for Asians in Hollywood. He believes that to bag a role which is not specific to his color or the way he speaks or acts is very difficult and if it all he does a Hollywood film; his role should be well crafted with dignity to make India proud.

The actor appreciates the Indian personalities doing well on the International arena. It is a commendable thing. It is an experience. Beyond that, he does not think it is prerequisite or requirement for an actor or anyone from the Indian film Industry to do so that India becomes a bigger film Industry.

"As a kid in Delhi, I said something very stupid. I said 'if Bombay comes to me, I'll work in films.' God gave me that chance, people called me from there. I am not saying this with pride; I am saying this with the innocence of a kid. When I say I would like Disneyland to come to my doorstep. If Hollywood comes here, we will definitely make a movie and we will win," He said. In the same way, Hollywood have to come in India to cast him in a movie and he does not say this with any arrogance. It is a question of his belief and how he lives by it.

Shahrukh Khan does not make films to become an International star. His first step in the International Cinema was when he made his first film *Deewana* (1992). He has a belief that he became an International star when he gave his first shot for the Indian film Industry. He does not need any other justification or better qualification to be an International star. He is quite happy doing Hindi films. His dream would be to make a Hindi film, which is watched internationally. He thinks that the only way he can show thankfulness to the Indian film Industry is by making a pure Indian film and taking it to all over the world."I would like to make an Indian film which is loved internationally, rather than trying to get into an international film, and be loved because it's an international film," he said. That is the kind of dream he has and he tries to work towards doing that. The dream is not really to get into a Hollywood film.

Fans

Shahrukh Khan rules over the hearts of numerous fans all around the world. He is a part of their lives. Everybody feels his love and the maximum love he gives is to the people who watch him on the cinema. It is not easy to define the love of Shahrukh Khan to his billions of fans. They are the people who appreciate his work. He has conquered the heart of his fans with his love and respect for his profession. There is no word to describe the madness of his fans towards him. The euphoria that he creates among them is unparalleled.

He has all the goodness of media and fans. More than money, name and fame, what he earned is lot of love of his fans. He gets strength from the unconditional love and support from his fans. Wherever he goes, he engages with them with keen interest and excitement. This direct one to one made him feel even closure to all his fans. The love of his enthusiastic fans feels to him like love of someone very close to him. He can never have an ego or any kind of dis-regard for the love and goodness they gave him. He feels very important to connect with fans. There is oneness that people feel with him, which is beyond the entertainment that he gives them.

Shahrukh Khan has fans across different age barrier. He tries to make films, which everyone enjoys. He got the opportunity to work with people who appeal to different age groups. He loves and respect women because he thinks that women have brought him up, from his mother to his little daughter. As far as intelligent filmmakers are concerned, he has worked with very good thinking people in his career and he has put all his learning into his films. At last, he is like a child.

Khan's fans adore him because he has a respectful personality not only as a star but as a human being also. He has not changed a lot in years. The stardom does not affect him so much. His human touch is still there. Many people relate with him because of his background and journey to become star. He shares it with people openly. He is not ashamed of it. That is what makes people relate to him as a human differently. People feel from the heart and talk very personal about him. They write beautiful messages to Shahrukh Khan. They write about incidents, which have changed their life after watching his films. They think of him with lot of ownership. For them, he is the face of India to the world and one of the India's unofficial brand ambassadors. He has created a truly devoted and united fan base all across the world. He has been showered with love across national and cultural boundaries. His International fan following and recognition is admirable. He has been able to cross boundaries of language. He has great number of fans from all over the world who do not understand Hindi at all but still they love his movies. In countries like England and America, People of Indian origins are dedicated Shahrukh Khan Fans.

Shahrukh Khan's seaside mansion is a well-known place in Mumbai. Thousands of fans and well-wishers gather there every weekend to see him waving from the balcony. In a sense, it is a kind of acknowledgement. It is a way of telling Shahrukh Khan that he has been entertaining well for last many years. The actor feels very humble when he meets the people outside his home. He knows how to reciprocate his love and affection to them. He waves out to them when he is at home. He never dress up for these occasions. It just makes him feel very good and loved. "On weekend, I have hundreds of people outside my house. I feel like going and meeting them all. My security with guns says 'don't', but I want to meet them because I have to thank them. I think Fans are like how you feel in front of an ocean. You know, sometime when you are full of yourself you go down on a beach and stand in front of the sea and realize how insignificant you are. All the important (things) in your house your well coaster rooms, your Louis Vuitton, and your BMWs. You are like- oh God! I am so powerful. Then, you go and stand in front of the Sea and realize you are such an insignificant. Fans, to me, are like that sea. When I see them, I realize my insignificance without them. I want to go and stand with him and say ok I am insignificant but thank you for making me so significant, for making me so special," he said. This is the closest way anyone gets to see him and he does not feel any iconic status because of this. It shows his humility and goodness towards his fans.

Shahrukh Khan considers himself as an employee of his devoted fans. "I don't like calling people fans because I find it derogatory. I think I like to call them my employers. They are my employers," He is very humble about the fact that many people across the globe like him. He respects the fact that a major part of his life exists because of all the love and goodness people show to him. He is very clear that when he is with people, his life is for them. He feels genuine interest in his fans. He understands and feels the emotion of his fans and people who admire him. He can do anything to make them happy. Therefore, whether he is happy or sad, he can still make a lakh people smile. In goodness or sadness, he waves out to them and gives them a reason to smile. "That's what an actor's life is. It does not make a difference what I am feeling, I have to make you feel entertained when you meet me, when you see me, when you experience me," he said.

On 2 November, many people around the world celebrate his birthday. People from different corners of the world gather outside Shahrukh Khan's house to pay respect and catch a glimpse of their favorite star on his birthday. They think of it as a special day for themselves. He comes to wave-out them and lends a smile on their faces. He dances for them. He meets everyone with lot of love and humility. He feels a lot of goodness in doing that. He does it because he does not know how else to share the love with them. He celebrates his birthday only with the fans and media. He feels that there could not be a better way to celebrate his birthday than with so many people.

Being ordinary

Shahrukh Khan is a great believer of Ordinariness- a characteristic one does not usually expect from a celebrity who is a super star in the Hindi film Industry. He comes from a very normal middle class background and being a movie star, he has been treated very special. Therefore, he has seen both sides of the world but he considers himself a very ordinary person. He truly believes that he is leading a common life like everybody else. He thinks and does things like an ordinary man. In his own eyes, he is a hero because he is completely ordinary. There is nothing abnormal or special about him. By the virtue of profession, the work he does and the heights that people have placed him, he seems like a special person but he feels completely ordinary from the inside. He is like everyone else. He has a normal middle class upbringing that is present even now in his home with his children and wife.

Movie stars look very glamorous and special from outside. They enjoy a status quite unlike that of any other but the actor believes he has all the qualities of a man who is not a Public figure. He enjoys the smallest and the simplest pleasures of life with the same gust and happiness that are meant to enjoy. He has made films in which he talked a lot about ordinariness. That is what he has tried to keep in his films, in which he acts. His biggest belief in life is "it is not special to be special, it is special to be ordinary." According to him, It is very difficult to be that person who gets up early in the morning, takes a local train to his work, sits on a small little desk somewhere in his office, typing on his computer, getting back again in a crowded local train, comeback to his family, meet his children and really enjoy the festivals of *Diwali* and *Eid*. They enjoy more than the greatest or richest people in the world do. Khan wonders how does he do that. How is he able to be so full of life with that small amount of money?

"I am nothing great. I came from Delhi to get some work, do a few song and dance routines and then to receive so much love and honor. If we try and remember that where we came from is our root, that's what we are, we'll be a lot happier in life," he said. Nothing is better than the ordinary Life we lead. He has realized this after working so many years in the Hindi Film Industry and he can say with experience to every youngster "If you remember where you came from, your roots you will be far happier and you will also get name and fame but you are happiest when you remember your roots."

He feels that until we have a human trait that we can fail, till then we are completely ordinary. He has the same fear of failure today as when he started working in Hindi cinema and keeps tirelessly working to overcome that fear. "One of the things that we all face in life is failure and I try not to become a failure in spite of failing very often. I still have the same fear as I did the first day I started working. I think I will continue to have a fear that I should always succeed, try and do the best that I can," he said by adding that "I keep working because I also know that as long as I keep working, as long as I keep believing, I'll be able to overcome all my failures."

Majority of people struggle to live a regular and normal life. They struggle, strive and still live life in happiness and sadness. They try to overcome all the issues of daily life by meeting everything ahead first. They achieve so much in life with a little facility at hand. They have nothing special to say and share. That is the beauty of a common person. They inspire Shahrukh Khan. People, in his humble opinion, become special by choices rightly made or just by virtue of something going right in their life, which they also do not know. Everyone appreciates these people but the common man has the ability to look really beyond all the problems and issues that they face every day and every life. That makes them a real hero. He believes that he should retain that ordinariness around him to achieve a little more in life.

He works for fulfilling some amount of happiness for ordinary people through the cinema that he does. He dedicated his life to make as many common people as he can. Whenever he makes a public appearance, he tries his best to share some love and Entertainment with them.

Shahrukh Khan believes that the nicest thing that ordinary People can have in life is that they are alive. It is the greatest belief or strength of normal people that they realize every day and thankful just to be alive. He likes to have a nice life. He likes to be happy. He likes to smile more often than cry in a day. He is a very ordinary human being. A very basic and simple thing makes him happy and enjoys life. He believes that ordinary people can become the most special people if they keep working hard and have big dreams.

Winning is Important

Shahrukh Khan gets disturbed when he does not win. He believes in the saying, which is very greedy that "Losing is not an option". In his write-ups and interviews, he may say loses teach you how to be a resilient. It teaches us patience. It teaches us how to be better but he hates to lose. He does not like it. He hides his expressions under his wonderful dimpled smile but he feels extremely sad when he loses any game.

He is over-sensitive. He cannot handle loses very easily. He cried when his team Kolkata knight riders lost nine matches in a row in South Africa. He cried shamelessly in bathroom for days and felt very disappointed. That was the worst phase of his life because he felt he disappointed his children. Everything that could go wrong was going wrong. Every action that they did, every player that they chose, every move that they made just went wrong. There were several reasons by which they lost. He did not expect his team to do so badly. In his line of work, he never let down an audience. For the first time in his career, he started thinking, "Are we letting down people."

In movies, good or bad happens in two and half hours and then everything is happy. However, in real life, it is longer than just two and half hours. Sometimes it takes months or years but the actor never loses hope. "It distresses me. It kills me within any kind of lose but it doesn't kill me enough to not realize that when the win will come, that feeling and that euphoria will overcome any lose that you have experienced. I live by that," he said. He keeps patience, and most importantly, belief. He believes there is nothing more important than belief in life. If you have a belief that this is going to happen, it will happen. You should live with that belief.

Politics: A Self-Sacrificing job

In India, anyone can enter into Politics. Many people might consider it as a dirty pond but several film stars are entering into Politics since they have already get fame, recognition and money. It is apparently the place for many actors. However, it is hard to believe for many people that stars enters into Politics with the desire to serve the society but Shahrukh Khan is not on the same path.

Khan has an immense amount of regard and love for people and leaders who run the country. He has a huge amount of respect for Politicians, and believes that it is a profession, which needs to be respected the most. He knows most of the Politicians and discusses many things with them but by nature, he is completely apolitical. He never wants to join the mainstream politics. He has been too long in the Entertainment field to change it. The actor believes in all the things, which an Indian should believe but he is not an expert in Politics. According to him, he is still trying to be an actor and serve the audience in that field.

He truly believes that Politics is too self- sacrificing. A Professional Politician should be happy with his life so that he or she can work for people. Most of the people in Politics are there to serve social causes than self-interest. It requires a lot of selflessness to run a country, a state or a small region. He is too used to a life, which is just about him and his family. He is too much in love with himself. He does not think that he can sacrifice his personal gains. He is too business oriented to be that Selfless.

Goals: Mere milestones

A wise man once said, "It is not the destination, but the journey that counts," this is certainly applies to Shahrukh Khan.

The actor has never worked for posterity or future. He just works for the next moment. On the professional front, he has never thought he has achieved everything in life. There is a long way to go. When he started his career in the Hindi film Industry, he did not have targets. He does not believe in destinations or retirement. He has never designed or managed what is going to happen. He truly believes that filmmaking is Creative and Creation cannot bound by restrictions. It should free flowing. "I have not thought of any destination. I always say that I don't work for posterity or prosperity. I don't work to be remembered except by my kids. I work because I love to work. I like the process of waking up in the morning, and I feel shy to say, put on makeup, go quickly and act. If I have not done well the day before, I want to do better and if I do a great job before; I want to do that again. That's all. It's simple and straightforward as that," he said.

Khan further continued, "I don't see an end. I want to tell the youngsters that if you keep a goal in mind as a standard what happens when you reach that. There is no finish line in my race. I want to keep running. So I don't have an end in sight, I just want to do better."

Many People say that you need to know where you are going and need to be determined about reaching there. However, it has not been the case with Shahrukh Khan. He has never set goals. He has never set out to earn a particular amount to count the crores at the box office or to compare his worth with anyone else. In his opinion, "Quantifiable goals are indeed illusion". The only reality is hard work. "I never knew my destination. I can't even claim to know it today. Now that I am on the covers of Forbes India; Is that where I wanted to be as a businessman? My IPL team has won the championship and it's profitable; is that the dream I had for a sporting franchise venture? I have a film running on a cinema hall for the last twenty years; should that be the attempt in terms of achievement for my next film? No, I don't think so. I believe goals actually limit your ambition and desire. I don't mean that you don't have goals but call them mere milestones. Think of them as a passing moment of excellence and keep on striving harder for a place, which cannot be defined or confined by names and numbers", he said at IIMB Leadership Summit 2015.

Shahrukh Khan has hunger or greed to keep on doing more work. He is restless. He does not have an ending inside. He does not have a place to arrive. He still has a long way to go. He is like a mountain climber who is not going for the peak. He does not want to reach the end. He wants to keep climbing and it is not for ambition, greed and for success. It is just for the want of climbing. "I walk, I run, in the direction of my dreams. Things change along the way, people change, I change, the world changes even my dreams change. I don't have a place to arrive. I just keep doing what I know how to do the best that I can do it," he told the youngsters at Yale University.

2

Talking Traits

The exhilarating journey of Shahrukh Khan, from Television serials, to films, to producer, to entrepreneur has required a huge amount of potential, caliber and strength. He has certain sensibilities on which he sticks. He has always known the fact that if you don't have the guts, you don't get the glory. The demographics of Khan's fan following depends a lot on his traits. He influences and inspires people by his personal qualities. He has several traits for being a truly global Indian Legend.

A Hardworking Actor

Shahrukh Khan is an achiever. He has achieved a number of milestones in his career. Apart from several achievements, he has been successful in his work related to the Entertainment Industry but this is not a happenstance. The actor strongly believes in hard work. His stardom and achievements are supported by tremendous hard work and acting potential. If there is one simple value that describes Shahrukh Khan, that captures his fascinating journey and what he stands for, it has to be his burning dedication to work extremely hard. He has a reputation of being one of the most hardworking man in Hindi film Industry. People love the spirit and honesty with which he works. Due to this quality, he is respected everywhere. He does not have enough talent. He believes his talent is limited as compared to the actors, singers, writers and directors around him but he tries to cover it up by working hard. A person can learn from the excessive hard work that he does that there is a life, which can only happen if you have goodness and hard work in your heart.

Individually, he works hard for every film in his own space. He has always said that, "When I am giving a shot, I always believe this is my first shot. So, I am as nervous as a new comer would be and I also believe I won't get another chance. This is my last shot." He has that humility and importance attach to that moment.

The journey of the actor has genuinely taken him beyond what he dreamed of, though he had no dreams. When he started his career, he never thought of any end or result. He never thought of earning huge amount of money. He did not want to win number of awards or to do number of films. He just wanted to do work. There is no end line to his work. He never thought of himself anywhere but in front of camera. He never says he is tired. He does not want to take time off. The concept of 'Sundays off' does not mean anything to him. He travels long distances to get a very little. He pushes himself day and night without sleep and put a lot of effort so that he can say 'thank you' to all the people who has given him the opportunity to act. He wants to pack as much as he can in a day through hard work. He does not plan or strategize things for future. His idea is to wake up in the morning, do the work given to him, return home and then start all over again the next day. When he does not work, he gets sad, depressed and lonely.

Shahrukh Khan, the Bollywood mega star, gives the impression of doing several things at a time whether it is work, business or family. Everyone wonders how he manages at all. He loves his work. He adores the fact that he is an idol of many young Indians. Old women think of him as their son. He feels it is the gift of God and he needs to fulfill it. Therefore, he works for the smile of these people in spite of having so many problems- Personal, Professional or Physical. He keeps working harder to get more hugs and smiles from the people who love him.

Shahrukh Khan has a strange passionate drive towards doing things. He strongly believes in doing. He believes in not knowing may be but he is happy not knowing as long as he is doing. "May be that's what God made us for: just go and do. In this world, 'just go and do' is like sending you to Euro Disney. Just go and enjoy the rides. Just have a good time. Don't worry how it works. Don't think about what's happening. I want every Indian to believe that. Just enjoy the ride, have a good time. Do things. go wrong. You know, sometimes you feel sick of the ride. It's ok to feel a bit sick. It is all right. Just do it so that you have the full experience of Life and come back," Khan said.

He feels proud to say 'I don't know'. He wants to teach his children the ability to tell their parents and teachers with pride that 'I don't know'. He follows that maximum. "I want every youngster, at least my children; I want them the capacity, the guts, the honesty and the innocence to turn around and say 'I don't Know,' he said.

He has achieved all the goodness and luxuries of life just by doing and by knowing very little. He does not know many things and ready to learn. He is so keen to learn from the everyday life. He finds it all right if somebody knows a little because he believes there is life to teach him or her. There is life to take so much. The lesser you have, there is more to get. It is good to be greedy for knowledge and life. "It's all right not to know. It's all right to make mistakes. It's all right to go wrong because that's what life is meant for and enjoy it. Don't do and destroy yourself decidedly so. Just do what makes you happy and I can assure you with my experience of many losses, many failures, many wrongs that at the end of it all, it will be very happy and if it is not happy like I said in my film it's not the End," Khan mentioned.

Shahrukh Khan tries extra hard to entertain people. He always put extra effort to give people what they want from him. At the end of his career, he wants to be known as an actor who tried because he works very hard. He believes that it is difficult to be a star but it is impossible to remain there unless you are trying very hard. He has a greed for life. "Oh I am very greedy. I am ambitious. I have read somewhere and I believe that if you let go off greed, you might as well stop loving. People assume that greed is only for money or material stuff but there is greed for everything. I have greed for life. In the last 10 years, I have pushed in 20 years. In my last film, I pushed in three films. In my last shot, I pushed in 18 shots and I still make it look effortless but I think I have very little time on this earth because I have seen too many things which I thought were permanent, go just like this whether it's my parents, whether it's the business whether it's me being in Delhi," he said.

He further continued, "Good things go like this and bad things go like this. They just go. I am not afraid of this. I am not saying I will die tomorrow or something but I think I have a very little time and I want to push as much as I can in that. That is the greed. I am a great believer of Allah and God. When I go to god, he asks me Listen! I send you to earth and I want to know what already you do. I want to answer him back and say ask me what I did not do. That will be easier"

Every morning he wakes up with the desire in his heart to surprise people with the work. The actor has believed that the ability to surprise people who love him so much for many years is actually more difficult. That is one of the biggest losses of being successful and consistently working that they lose the ability to surprise people. Even the best is sometimes not good enough. So as a creative person, it is a challenge for him to always do new things in the fixed parameters of commercial cinema and make things better than the previous one."When you are extremely successful, you lose the ability to shock people. You lose the ability to surprise people because everybody expects the unexpected from you already. You lose the ability so you have to try extra hard," He observed. Therefore, he wants opportunities from people so that he still be able to surprise them.

An Energetic Star

The most extra-ordinary thing about Shahrukh Khan is his Energy Level. He is considered as the most energetic personality in the Indian film Industry. He has a unique energy level that cannot match by everyone. People admire his incredible Energy. His screen image is full of vitality. He can go on without sleep for long hours.

Shahrukh Khan does so many different things at the same time but his energy never run slow. He cannot be at rest. He remains energetic and full of life all the times. He likes going out of the house every day and trying to make things happen. He is not someone who stays at one place while working. He is energy in motion. He always keep doing and thinking. He enjoys the process of working so much that he does not feel tired. "I like to fill the space. You know I don't want to be a part of the space. I don't want to be part of atmosphere. I want to be the atmosphere," he quoted once. He likes an active lifestyle. The only thing that he does not like taken away from him is his energy and active lifestyle.

An Anti-Social actor

Shahrukh Khan is a Bollywood star who never fails to impress the audience with his dimple, quick wit and innate sense of humor but a little known fact about this dazzling superstar is that he is a shy person in personal life. The actor considers himself shy of women and new people. When he relates with them, he has a little bit of shyness. He is not easy with them. He likes to be his own. He does not know how to interact with a woman because he studied in a segregate school. He does not do the regular interaction that normally men does with women. He cannot go to a party. He cannot stand with people. He cannot travel alone. He does not know how to be socially interactive with people. His mother used to call him anti-social.

In acting, an actor needs to expose a lot. He needs to express emotions and dialogues. He has to come out and be in the open. Through acting, he does all things that he cannot do in real life. It has become a huge gift for him that he can be somebody else. He can go and do something without feeling responsible for that. Therefore, he acts to cover up his awkwardness.

The actor has replaced loneliness, depression and people with work in life. He has surrounded himself with so much work because when he works, he met many people and interacts with them through this common goal. He does not interact with them socially. "Many of my filmmaking colleagues complain that after the film is over, you don't talk to us. I can't explain to them. I don't have anything else to say. I love you. I miss you but I miss you through the work," He said. He loves many people like family but he cannot socialize with them. He hates being with them at times.

He feels very odd with them. He cannot sit and chat with them. He is not like how he is in his movies especially in romantic parts. While working, he can just be with them.

Shahrukh Khan has been accepted in a nice manner by huge amount of people for the goodness of work that he does. He lives for that goodness. He can do anything to make them entertained. A part of him just wants to do that and a part of him just wants to be alone at times because he feels that if he is not reclusive and strange, he would not be able to work very hard.

A Supremely Disorganized Person

People ask the Indian actor Shahrukh Khan what he sells. Does he sell expressions? Does he sell stardom? Does he sell Brands? No! He sells Time. His time is precious. He tries to finish work on time. He makes sure that anyone who is working with him gets what he desires. He tries to give them value for money.

In addition, the actor is not conscious about coming on time but he is a punctual person unless he is working which is a lot of time. His presence in places is what matters to people. He has reached at a level where he has to end-up and land-up at places. He just has to walk in and walk out. Whenever he is asked about his punctuality, he pompously says, "Time starts when I reach somewhere." He works round the clock. There are so many demands on him because he manages to do so many things at a time. Everyone wants to consume a part of him in a good sense and he does not like saying "No". This is what he is made to do.

He is not governed by Time. He hates being bound by organizers. He has maintained that time does not control you. He is completely unbound by time and this is something on which he is proud. In his opinion, "Time starts when I come to a place. So I am not bound by time, otherwise I would never manage. I am never on time for meetings and I am very proud of it or at least I am not ashamed of it. I am disorganized about time but I know I manage to meet 85,000 people in a year. Genuinely, I am able to talk to about 45 filmmakers in a year. I am able to do three films in a year. I am able to spend great quality time with my children. I am able to give full attention to my wife and my sister. I am able to do everything that I wish to do also. So I have actually, in a certain sense, conquered time, which makes me feel sometimes that I may even, conquer death, but that won't happen. That I know realistically but I have conquered time,"

Being a Role Model

Shahrukh Khan is one of the biggest stars in Bollywood arena. He is a motivational leader. He is successful in the art of influencing and motivating people. Anything he says does have a massive impact on the mind-set of people. He has many credentials for being a Role model. He has captured the imagination of youth India and his success from a Muslim middle class to heartthrob is true inspiration for them. He became one of the biggest Bollywood star completely on his own terms. People say that many young people looks up to him because he keeps going on and use high level of excellence. He represents high moral beliefs that influence the behavior, attitude and philosophy of people. He represents everyday man in India who has a dream to become a Bollywood star and he has done so successfully that he gives younger generation a hope and a feeling that if he can do it, maybe they can do it too. In a way, He has positively touched the lives of many people, across several sections of society. His lives and actions have enriched their lives. One can learn the way to live life by following him. He is a role model or icon for the Indians across all social classes.

The Shahrukh Khan phenomenon does not have an age barrier or gender barrier. He has managed to inspire people of several generations. He has a significant impact on large number of people. There is a responsibility, which comes on him, having reached a certain stage of success. He is such a huge star that the smallest things that he says can affect people's life. His thoughts, beliefs, and emotions influence young people as well as people of other generations. He has something that does not reflect anywhere else in the world but he does not have the best habits.

The actor, often credited as the king of Bollywood, is a chain smoker. He has often caught with a cigarette in public, though he is well aware of the fact that Smoking is injurious to health. He has confessed that it is the "worst habit" anyone can have. He does not like it and he wants to give it up. Therefore, he does not advocate smoking to anyone.

When asked about smoking in films in an interview with Karan Thapar, a noted television interviewer, the Delhi born actor said, "I won't belittle it by saying that smoking is artistic in films, and that's why we are having this problem. But the whole larger issue is today smoking, tomorrow what? And where does it go ahead? It's an art form and it should be left alone and I think and truly believe that the Indian masses are literate enough that there is no more any Humphrey Bogart kind of smoking now - that you will start smoking because an actor does and it's a very small health issue. I think the powers should look at bigger health issues than smoking in films."

Former Health Minister Dr Ambumani Ramadoss had often mentioned that Shahrukh's habit of smoking publicly sets a bad example for youngsters. He argued that he is also against smoking scenes in movies as this too has bad influence on the audience especially on teenagers. He, also, appealed him not to advertise soft drinks.

The megastar responded, "I would appeal to any authority like that to ban it. Don't let it sell in our country if it is bad for children. If smoking is bad, don't let production in this country. My logic is you are not stopping it because it gives you revenue. Let's be honest about it. You are not stopping certain products if you think that they are harmful, but they earn revenue to the government. Then don't stop my revenue, I am an actor. I am supposed to do a job and get revenue from it. Very clearly, if you think something is wrong, stop making it. There is no problem with that."

People claim he is a role model or a Public figure. However, he does not consider himself as a role model. He wants everyone to know very clearly that he is not a role model. He did not set out to be a role model. He wanted to be a movie star and act in front of a camera. "I am an actor and an entertainer. I am not supposed to be a role model for youngsters and if they want to make me one, it is at their own risk. I don't have the best habits in the world. I don't sleep enough hours. I don't eat properly. I smoke. These are all bad things and I wouldn't like any youngster to do them," He said.

In terms of work, he might be a role model but personally, he is very different. He never behaves like a role model. He thinks of them as people who play a role according to the perception that people think of them. He truly believes that he cannot be insincerely humble because he is a public figure. He can make mistakes. He can be wrong. He likes young people to know that be yourself from wherever you are. Most of the time being myself means being happy.

3
The Speed of Thoughts

We are familiar with the maxim that "he Came he saw and he conquered," but "he came he spoke and he conquered" certainly applies to the Badshah of Bollywood Shahrukh Khan.

Bollywood icon Shahrukh Khan is an entertainer as well as an eloquent speaker. Over the years, He has been a regular speaker at Public events, Discussion forums and gathering of intellectuals. He wears business suit and represent an image of a 'gentleman.' His speeches are precise and make a spectacular impact on the listeners. He deeply influences them with his words and clarity of thoughts.

He speaks very well and it shows in his various interviews and Press conferences. He is arguably the best conversationalist in Bollywood. He has been noted for several gestures and ways of delivering superbly crafted speeches in his own characteristic style. He features regularly in serious discussions. He is known for his words and superstardom. He expresses his thoughts in a very respectful manner. People like his oratory skills and the way he puts his thoughts together before others. He does not speak for the sake of speaking, whatever he says is invariably convincing and to the point. A maturity in his thoughts makes him a master orator.

Beyond the obvious skills of acting and dancing, he is skilled at connecting with his various audiences. As a well-informed Indian, He embraces audience with his contemporary style of speaking. He always seems at ease with himself and comfortable while speaking to a large audience. Apart from voice and good look, the greatest personality about Shahrukh Khan is his immense amount of education, which helps him to connect with the audience. His presence in Public dealings project self-confidence and supreme self-belief, which comes by education that carries around him.

The most fascinating thing about Shahrukh Khan is that he is a rare combination of Success and intelligence. He is an intellectual giant. He is known for giving intellectual answers to the questions in any interview or intellectual gathering. He is a congenial personality when it comes to media interaction and press conferences. He gives long answers. He elaborates his opinion very well. Every statement that he makes is well thought. His interviews are full of valuable thoughts and forthright views that affect people's feeling and belief. He inspire people with his noble thoughts, which are always positive and often deeper than his movies. He loves to share the experiences and stories about life with everyone in simpler words. As a well-informed Indian, he tells everyone what he believes and what works for him. He never afraid to say anything that he wants to. He has the guts to be so direct and truthful about the experience and perspective on life. It's, definitely, a skill that is honed by observing the world around. The audience trusts his words and follows his suggestion.

Through interviews, he propagates right message to the society. He does not only talk about the philosophy of life, he talks about the reality of life. He talks very wisely and flaunts many things. He speaks very fast. His mind works very fast. He amazes everyone through his ability of thinking and speaking quick and so fast. He actively participates in various television shows and likes to voice meaningful thoughts and opinion. Whatever he learned in childhood from his parents, teachers and friends- all these incredible experiences come in handy. In a way, he did not enter in the Indian film Industry when he was 18-19 years old. He was 26 by the time he started. Thus, he had already lived one-fourth of his life. He had a lot of enriching positive and negative experiences, which he does not mind sharing with people.

Shahrukh Khan's speeches are known for mixing serious discussions with humor. He has mastered the tough task to give intelligent statements and being funny at the same time. His talks are full of humor and he has the ability to look cheerful all the times. He touches the heart and minds of people through the ability to use the words in an amusing and imaginative ways. With a wacky sense of humor, he knows to give right answer to every question. As an entertainer, he finds things very positive in life. He laughs at odd things which people find stressful. He finds things very funny. He sees the funny part of things rather than seeing the stressful part that means glass is always half full for him not half empty.

He is so relevant and interesting. He does the stuff that comes naturally and never tries to be something else. He believes that to be relevant, you have to be yourself and aware of the things that are happening. He is a voracious book reader. He has yearning for learning. He keeps learning about new things in life. He has curiosity for life and people. He wants to get informed about various things and being an actor, it comes naturally to be aware of the things that are happening.

Shahrukh Khan's life is an open book when it comes to media. He talks openly. He jokes openly but there is a part of him, which he has been able to cover up and hold back. The actor is an entertainer. Whenever an actor comes on a public platform, his only desire is that the audience has a good time when they meet him. Under all that, he has wrapped a very personal and private part of him, which nobody knows. Lot of things has gone in his life, which he has never openly talked. Genuinely, there is a part of his way and thinking which nobody knows not even his children.

The Twitter Bandwagon

Shahrukh Khan is a very active user of micro-blogging site Twitter. He has a very strong presence on Twitter. He has an amazing number of followers from all over the world, which keeps increasing. He joined the online platform in January 2010 and received rapturous Welcome. "Once I came on, I was just looking at the Laptop and suddenly I had, I think, 900 or 1000 people joining me. I was very touched. The only thing that humbles me in life is how can people like me so much. It's very humbling. I can't explain it," he said by adding "Everyone talks about my stardom to 15 years. What keeps you grounded and blah...blah...blah, but the real reason is that I can't imagine people who don't know me, care about me so much and they say nice things. It's very selfless and once people started writing, I am like listen! Now I cannot stop replying."

Khan shares very personal things with his followers. He shares thoughts, film-updates, and fun moments of life with them. His tweets are meant for everyone. Some people claim that he is too intellectual there but he writes and express thoughts on such platforms because he feels them and there are certain nice things that he can say. He often gets philosophical there. He talks about the hopefulness of life. He likes to narrate a lot of feelings and thoughts that he thinks during his reclusive time through Twitter. He also concludes interactive sessions with his fans. Social networking sites are full of youngsters. He likes sharing his experience with youth because he believes in youth and stands for them.

Freedom of speech and expression

Shahrukh Khan is a Public figure. He is in the business of entertainment. He belongs to an area or work, which truly believes in the freedom of speech and expression. He is quite comfortable in exposing many genuine real-emotions in public. He is a person who likes to speak his mind. He is a person with a viewpoint and quite honest about his opinion. He likes to make a comment and take stands. People appreciate what he writes and speak as a public figure.

People, sometimes, ask his political and religious views. They want to know his opinion on issues. They ask him questions pointed and directed to things, which he does not appreciate but by the power of his vast knowledge and dazzling smile, he still answers them with lot of fun and happiness. He tries to entertain them with his answers. This shows his ability to tolerate the nonsense with a smile on the face. The main thing about his job is to be magnanimous about sharing love with everyone, which includes the media and people watching him on television or anywhere else. He has some wonderful answers if people have good enough questions. However, he has found that, sometimes, sharing of personal thoughts gets misinterpreted, misread or misunderstood. He has learned that when a public figure expresses himself or herself, they open themselves for discussion- positive or negative. People attach a lot of weightage to what he says. He writes something, then it becomes news, and sometimes taken as something he did not mean it. It becomes a slogan. When he or any other public figure makes a comment on a serious issue, it is noticed beyond the importance it should be given and their personal point of view or simple answer is more important than the people who know it better.

Shahrukh Khan is a very sensitive and emotional person. He has reached at a stage in life where he does not find some of the things very funny and when he tries to say something funny; it is taken as wrong too. Therefore, it is a losing battle.

In 2010, Shahrukh Khan, co-owner of Kolkata Knight Riders franchise, lands himself into trouble when he spoke about the non-inclusion of Pakistani players in the Indian Premier League. He was asked to make an apology for his views that Pakistani players should be allowed to play in the IPL but he refused to do so. Later, People from a political party attacks on the screenings of his film *My name is Khan* (2010). There are many such instances where he made a public comment and lands himself in some sort of controversy. Due to such incidents, he admitted that he has become a little wary of making political and religious remarks. In addition, many people in Hindi film Industry feel that way. Therefore, he does not speak his mind often enough because he worries that his film shooting will be cancelled for no reason. He has realized that what he says on a public platform has to be a little more cautious and clearly stated because he has been in a profession which is so related to always been talked about and scrutinize. Being a Public figure, most of his actions and intentions are reviewed and sometimes questioned. Each thing he says can hurt people. People say he has mastered the art of diplomacy but this is not diplomatic. He just speaks cautiously about issues because his impact of what he says is huge on common people especially on young people. He likes to stay away from things which he has no full knowledge or understanding. He cannot make a comment on things that are in the news for reason. He cannot speak on subjects, which do not include his area of work.

The actor has always believed that their personal thinking about any serious issue is same as any ordinary person. They have the same belief. He does not express his opinion as a joke. He really thinks that one needs to be a little more thoughtful. Not everything is a joke and just spice. There is life beyond that.

Quietness: the Soul of Life

There has been a phase of Shahrukh Khan's silence and there is great loudness and superstardom in his silence. He has believed that when there is so much written and talked about him, the best thing is to go quiet. "I never think anyone thinks negative about me but I have been feeling that with the kind of talk and things that I read or said about me at times, I started carrying different kind of emotions and manifestations of those emotions like anger, jealousy, hatred, disturbance sometimes even love, longing, passion," He said in a candid interview with director Karan Johar.

"I have realized this that with so many things to carry, with so many attachments, the journey of my life beckons to sound and feel very heavy. I don't want to have all these baggage of jealousy, anger and hatred. It's only humanly impossible to ignore some of the things, which are said about me. I notice lot of people using my name, I think, rather frivolously. I am like should I react to it.... I have decided not to have these baggages with me. I have decided to do this journey free of luggage. I want to just carry a handbag of my family, my friends, keep very little stuff on it, walk slowly, happily, on this beautiful life that Allah has given me. I think one of the step towards those losing of that baggage, even though its Louis Vuitton, is to just go a little quiet and be with myself for a while." He added.

He narrated a story from ancient Religious epic Ramayana. Once Hanuman was fighting with a person. The person kept on becoming big and hanuman kept on becoming big. Both becoming big. Suddenly when the person became gigantic, Hanuman just went very small. When he went small, it was very difficult for the person to catch on and fight with him. This is what quietness is. By way of this story, he has come out a truth in life that Quietness is the soul of life.

Charming Bad Boy Image

Shahrukh Khan, in his extensive career, has made headlines for wrong reasons too. He has seen himself embroiled with several controversies owing to either his statements or behavior. The actor has the image of politeness and courtesy all the times. When an actor or a public figure build, a huge and large personality then he almost become slave to it. He has to behave exactly as people expect. In a way, anyone can take advantage of the vulnerable position or situation of an actor or public figure because they no longer remain common people. It is one of the trappings of stardom.

He is a gentleman, educated, well brought up and has an image to live upon. He is not aggressive in nature. He never takes aggressive stands. He has become a person who accepts a lot. Being from the land of Mahatma Gandhi, he likes to resolve things with peace and understanding. He never let ego and false sense of self-respect come in the way of normal discussion.

Sometimes media person talks about his behavior in public. They present things about him like a joke. Sometime they talk rubbish. He gets sad and lonely. He cover it up with the façade of being humorous and having fun all the time but it hurts him. A part of being a star is coping with rumors about his behavior in public. All the good things that are said in media are exaggerated about Shahrukh Khan. All the bad things are also a little exaggerated about him. The truth lies somewhere in the middle and he knows that truth because he leads his life. "I am not as good as people make me out to be and I am not as bad as people make me out to be. I am somewhere in the middle and it's difficult for people to gauge unless they know me," he said. Shahrukh Khan also belongs to the field of media and entertainment. He believes that if they are working on the same plane, then there has to be some grace in the work that they do otherwise he can talk only about professional things and go away.

Every action or opinion of an actor gets scrutinize relentlessly. Many people analyze movie stars outside their line of work also. They, sometime, watch stuff on television and form opinions. They start building images of people watching the images on screen. Shahrukh Khan believes that as long as it is professional, he still can accept it but when it starts getting personal, he gets disturbed. "Sometimes I just want to tell people- you don't know me. You don't live the life I have. You never going to have the life that I do even if you become ten times the star that I am *inshallah*. Do not analyze an issue of mine which you see on public display," he said by adding that "Do not analyze it by giving characteristic out of my personal personality. If people are going to be careless about his personal life, then he disrespects that. If they do not respect his personal life, he also does not respect how he deals with them.

Shahrukh Khan has admitted that he is the employee of the image that he has created and that image is affable, happy-go-lucky, and always exuberant. He speaks the language of love and happiness. He is someone who speaks his heart and mind. He understands the power of images and quite aware of the fact that the controversial acts can affect his wholesome image. However, he does not take SRK's image seriously. He believes that if he starts taking himself too seriously, it takes away him being an entertainer. As an actor, whatever stardom he has is never taken seriously. He never tries to intellectualize what he does. He does not believe in perceptions. He never behaves like a star in public places. He never maintained the image that he portrays in his films that he has chosen to do. Therefore, He wants to tell everyone that do not give so much importance to him by talking about his meltdown, crisis and problems. It is just an image. However, when people make such analysis about him, he just put it down to top Psychology of people who have nothing better to do.

Here are some inspiring Shahrukh Khan quotes:

- Success is never final and failure can never be fatal.
- I work the dark until sunrise on most days and fall asleep as the world awakens to light. My friends call me an owl... I like to think of myself as Bat...Batman...the prince of darkness.

- Do not try to feed your stomach with creativity; it is food for your soul, not your stomach.
- I have always noticed that Greatness does not come just by being talented. I think Greatness comes if you put a lot of hard work and always believe that you can do better.
- There used to be a little flag I used to carry during the march past in my school: "Do your best and Leave the rest." I think it is a good philosophy of Life. You should just give your best shot to everything and let the other things be.
- Sports teaches you how to lose but it also teaches you how not to be a loser.
- You cannot win a silver. You only lose the gold.
- We got to be grateful to everyone who works for us works with us makes us who we are brings us to what we become because on your own I believe you are not unique you are just alone so Gratitude should be an attitude.
- Reality makes you open to doubt but Delusions keep the impossible in site. Black and white may be real but 2+2 being 22 is much more inspiring.
- If you fail once, don't worry, try again, learn from it. If you succeed once, Don't become hot headed and big headed.
- When you are most down, it is the best place to be because you can't go further. You can only go up.
- If you don't respect what you do, nobody is going to respect it back.
- If you don't wake up in the morning with the belief that you are the best, chances are you won't be even better. When I say I wake up in the morning and believe I am the best, it is to try and work towards an excellent level of best, hoping to reach it. If I don't at least be better or good.

4
Ladies First

Shahrukh Khan, India's most charismatic film star, symbolizes true Love. Through movies, he inspired people to follow the path of love. He is a big believer of relationship and people loving each other. He had portrayed love and romance with such excellence that he has become the heartthrob of millions of people. In Hindi Cinema, 1980s was the time of lot of aggressive films. The story mainly focused on the plight of poor, the actors were quite violent and rebellious but films had great entertainment value. The 1990s, when Shahrukh Khan started working in Hindi films, saw the return of romantic movies and he credited for popularizing this concept in Hindi Cinema.

During this time, he did a number of films in which the audience wanted to have a feeling of love. Most of the characters that he played were Romantic characters in films like *Dilwale Dulhania Le Jayenge* (1996), *Kuch Kuch hota Hai* (1998) and some others. These films were highly intense and portrayed a wide variety of emotions, which were connected, with the lives of people. It somehow makes him believe that Love is really a universal Language that everyone can relate too.

Once Shahrukh Khan asked a German Lady, "Why do you like Indian films?" She said, "We have a button for Escalator, we have a button for coffee, but we don't have a button for crying and feeling emotions. So Indian films makes us cry." He equated these things and find that love makes you cry. Togetherness of this, He found two universal truths about the whole human community around the world- they all love and they all cry.

Shahrukh Khan gave romantic films a reality where one could see the real colors of life. In addition, these films gave Hindi cinema a new identity overseas. Playing romantic characters is one of the major highlights of his filmy career. After featuring in utterly romantic love stories, he garnered with the tag of "Ultimate king of Romance." The way he played these characters, everyone became his fan. He made the audience teary eyed and told love is all that matters. His Dialogue delivery, facial expressions and demeanor made him one of the unique romantic actors of Hindi Cinema. These romantic characters were a great success not only in India but overseas also. The way he played the lover boy role in movies has raised the standard for future romantic actors.

The actor believes that the kind of film every actor chooses to do say something about him or her. Any self-aware actor will never do a film that is not an extension of his personality. In a way, Most of the Romantic films have done well for him because He lends some parts of his personality to the character. He treated woman very well in the film and during the process of filmmaking. More than personally, his storytelling has treated them equally. This is the one reason people think he is a good romantic hero.

The greatest qualities of actor Shahrukh Khan is his respect for women. He genuinely feels that there is God and after that, there is women- whether her avatar is that of a mother, sister, wife, friend, daughter, assistant or director. He is a gentleman towards every woman he meets. He truly and absolutely love them. His respect for life is because he is surrounded by so many women. They have brought him up. According to him, women are the most beautiful creation of God. He admires and appreciates their beauty. He has always believed that a woman's beauty is extremely special. It should appreciated with lot of respect. He finds it completely wrong if someone disrespect a woman in words, action and spirit.

For him, Romantic movies are not just about dancing with an actress or saying romantic lines to her. It is about giving respect to a woman. The maximum amount of respect that a woman can get is in terms of Love- whether it is from a son, lover, father, and brother or at a work place. He extends Romance to that level.

Whatever he does, basically, is respect for woman in the end. His genuine respect for women shows that he is unquestionably a great human being. He treats women with so much dignity. For him, love to a woman is dignifying her. He believes that a woman only needs to be dignified by her man and he tries his best to dignify every woman he meets.

In several Indian societies, men and women are treated differently. Often men enjoys more freedom than women do. The actor demands more freedom for women. He wants more power, strength and freedom to women to make the choices and do the things that they want to do. They should allowed pursuing studies and working outside home without going against the ideologies and culture. "I really believe that women are going to take this country forward, the world forward and I truly believe that they should have a little more freedom from their houses, from the thoughts without going against the culture or, you know, the ideologies that the country has for man and woman. But I think the freedom just to believe that they can achieve and do things way beyond what they have done so far," Shahrukh Khan said at an event on India's 66th Independence day.

Shahrukh Khan, in his career, has worked with some of the most beautiful, intelligent, talented, kind and caring women of Hindi film industry. He truly believes that in the Indian film Industry, the real heroes are the leading ladies. He is highly impressed by their professionalism. They are hardworking, brave and great achievers. He has found that most of the women with whom he worked are very sensitive towards work. Their work is more difficult in the film industry. They are the backbone of the Indian film industry. He has learned a lot from these leading ladies. The respect he has for the leading ladies is so immense because they help him so much during the process of filmmaking. His stardom, since he started working in Hindi films, rest extremely heavily on the shoulders of his leading ladies. He personally feels that apart from the directors and the producers, the biggest part of his success goes to the women who have worked with him. Certain roles that he has done are only possible because he learnt a lot from his wonderful co-actresses. They have made him look as good as he is. He has been taken care by them. A big part of his stardom is because of them.

His all-leading ladies inspire him. He learnt Kindness, conscientiousness, tirelessness, management and professionalism from them. He thinks of himself very fortunate that he shares a great bond with all of them. "They have a completely different take on life. Their whole attitude towards work is something that genuinely has helped me to sustain my stardom," he said by adding that "I am really fortunate that I have seen three generations of actresses starting from Sridevi and moving on to Kajol and to Katrina [Kaif], Deepika [Padukone]. It is a great learning experience because of the fact that the three different kind of mindset that I have learned from and each one of them has a commonality of being hardworking of course and very beautiful but somewhere they are down to earth. Another thing that I have learned from women is that they are very giving and they are very humble about their work."

Celluloid Women

Since its inception, Hindi Cinema has been dominating by patriarchal ideologies. Questions has raised about the portrayal of female characters on screen. Their representation is not satisfactory at all. A female character always revolve around the male character who is central to the story. They are secondary to the male character. Woman of substance is missing from film's narration.

Shahrukh Khan observed that in the male dominated Hindi film Industry, somewhere all the credit given to the men. Despite working hard, women in Bollywood films does not get the due credit and the recognition that they deserve. People talk about the commercial success of the film. He believes that the women in the films are the real reason that these films have done well. They wear make-up, learn dancing and sometimes stand in front of the hero so that he can dance a little better. They stuck to their guns more rigidly and with more perseverance than men do.

In addition, the actor shows huge amount of respect for women characters in a film. As an actor or producer, it is his conscious decision that the woman's role as a protagonist has to be equally important to men's role. He strongly believes that it is not right to portray a woman as a submissive personality. A woman's treatment in a film should be top class. They should get roles in films matching their age, stature and talent. In movies of his own production, actresses play a central character. They are not simpering females. They are confident, well-treated and independent women with a mind of their own. He never prefer to work in a film in which the character of a woman is not rightly portrayed. He always says that the Indian filmmakers must show women with a greater character and strength. They should represent women in a more meaningful and humane manner.

Shahrukh Khan has always been associated with women centric campaigns, which he promotes aggressively. He has supported several Campaigns in the area of women rights and equalities. He honors them whenever he has given a chance in films, stage or theatre. He wants to do things for women that make them feel equal and nice. In March 2013, on International Women's day, he took an initiative to enable and empower the leading ladies of the Indian film Industry. He urged that he would have his leading ladies name appear before his name in future film credits. He shot an infomercial for TATA Tea's 'Jaago Re' Campaign in which he pledged that all films of his production will credit the female lead actress name first and also addressed the issue of people's attitude towards women in the society. He started this with the movie *Chennai Express*(2013) in which he teamed up with Bollywood female star Deepika Padukone. She was credited ahead of Shahrukh Khan in the movie. In that way, he created a space for the celluloid women in Indian Cinema.

The actor believes that this is not just a way of giving them respect; it is a belief. It is a way to make a point. It is an attempt to change the mindset of people towards women. It is just a regular thing to do and every filmmaker should do that. Keeping these thoughts in mind, he made a small beginning towards a big change.

5
Success and fear of Failures

Usha Uthup, a renowned Indian Playback singer Says, "When you read you begin with ABC, when you sing you begin with do re mi. when you think of success, you think of Shahrukh.

The Indian superstar Shahrukh Khan enjoys a very high level of success. He crossed one milestone after the other within the quickest possible time in the Indian Entertainment industry. People are surprised how Shahrukh Khan, an ordinary person and an outsider, succeeded in Indian film Industry in a big way. He has willpower and determination to succeed. His rise to success has become a metaphor and inspiration for many people around the world. His Success stories have been incorporating in many tabloids and newspapers. These stories are the stuff of millions of books. He has all the qualities of a successful man and the way he maintained a very high success rate is the most encouraging aspect of his career.

However, the actor does not count successes. He feels that talking about how to become successful is of no use because it never teaches us anything. Therefore, it is very boring to hear success stories. He truly believes that the true road to success is not the desire for success but a fear of failure. His response to failure that made him a successful actor. "I feel that talking about how to become successful is a waste of time...instead let me tell you very honestly...whatever happened to me happened because I have always been terrified of failure. I don't want as much to succeed as much as I don't want to fail. I come from a very normal lower middle class family. I saw a lot of failure. My father was a beautiful man and the most successful failure in the world. My mother also failed to stay with me long enough for her to see me become a movie star," he said while encouraging young people at Yale University, America in 2012.

"At an early age after my parents died... I equated poverty with failure. I just didn't want to be poor. So when I got a chance to act in films it wasn't out of any creative desire that I did so... it was purely out of the fear of failure and poverty," he added. According to him, Success is the worst teacher in the world. It can make you feel invincible.

In his successful career, he never set success as a benchmark. He knows this thing very well that if he does that; he will fail every day. After reaching at such great heights of success, he still wonders whether people will like his work or not. He always tries to move beyond that.

The actor scared of failing. He is scared of coming second. He has such a fear of failure that he works harder even when he does not need to. He works longer when he does not have to. However, at the same time, he believes that one should never forget a failure. If you forget the failure then you never succeed. One should remember failure at least not to repeat it. In his words, "The one that go wrong should never be forgotten. The one that go right have a life of their own and they should be forgotten. They will take care of themselves."

He does not mean that failure is fun and one should keep on making that but insists that one should experience fair amount of failure if they really want to succeed in life. His logic is that failure adds color in life. It is something that helps to move towards the goals in life. He is more proud of his failure than his achievements because his achievements are Professional that comes because of 100 or 200 people who works with him. The failures are his personality and none of them are Life threatening, Dangerous, mean, cheap, uneducated, vulgar, deceitful or dishonest.

Here is how failure helps Shahrukh Khan to move towards his goals in his own words.

- Firstly, it is not the absence of failure that makes you a success - It is your response to failure that actually helps to buffer the reverses that you experience. I personally have one response to failure - pragmatism – recognition and belief that if one approach does not work, then the other will or might.
- Failure also gives me an incentive to greater exertion - harder work, which invariably leads to later success in most cases.
- Repeated failure has taught me to stop pretending I am someone else. It has given me the clarity to stick to the things that really matter to me instead of distracting me from my core.
- Failure also gets you to find, who your real friends are. The true strength of your relationships only gets tested in the face of strong adversity.
- Overcoming some of my failures has made me discover that I have a strong will and more discipline than I suspected. It has helped me to have confidence in my ability to survive.

Elements of Success

Since Shahrukh Khan started his filmy career in the early 1990s. No one has gained more success than he has in the Entire Indian Entertainment Industry and he has no idea how. He never really understood the secret of his success. He never understood how he has become a big star. He does not know how he has attained a peak position in the entertainment field. He has never been able to pinpoint what made him so successful.

There is a well-known story, which he usually reads whenever he called to give a speech on Success.

Once a bank president asked the secret of his success.

"I make Right decisions," he said.

"How do you get to know how to make right decisions?" they asked.

"Experience," he said.

"Well, how do you get experience?" they asked.

"By repeatedly making the wrong decisions," he said.

Therefore, it is very difficult to explain the reasons of success.

As Shahrukh Khan does not know the reason of his success, he does not know what to do but he wants to stick to it, so the assumption is to wake up in the morning and do the stuff that entertains people. Besides that, he thinks of nothing else.

He is a firm believer of the fact that a person cannot acquire wisdom from success that is why it cannot be pass on. "Success is something that cannot be passed on. You cannot pass it on as an inheritance. The greatest of people, the most successful of people, perhaps, will never be able to teach their children or their subordinates or their colleagues how to be a successful as they were even if they tell them everything exactly how they did it," he observed.

He honestly believes that success is not a direct result of any action. Sometimes it happens accidently and one takes credit for that. Some of his initial films discarded by other actors at that time. He acted in them because the producer could not find anyone else to do them. He got them. He just happened to be in those films at right time and at the right age. He took care of the opportunities, things went right for him and he became a megastar.

Shahrukh Khan, while addressing young people at Bengali trust event in 2012, said:

- Sometimes the success that you get or the things that you get in life, you do not understand how important they are and how wonderfully best they are for you. Therefore, whatever happens to you in your line of work, in personal life please accept it as the will of God and that is the best thing for you.
- Nobody is going to ever take away from you, snatch away from you what you really deserve.
- Whether you get something or not keep working hard because there is no alternative to hard work.

6
Marketing without Pause

In Commercial Hindi cinema, the business of cinema has started to play a big role in the Indian film Industry. In the public, everybody is more concerned and bothered about box-office figure. Even the audience response can read from those collections. Therefore, Movie-marketing has become a very important aspect of filmmaking. It has a huge impact on the profitability of the film. It creates demand for the film. It ensures box-office collection. Several cinematic ventures do not work at the box-office due to lack of Marketing. So it has become important to create effective marketing campaigns and innovative promotional strategies in order to ensure good results at the box-office. It has become a vital component as like the script and content of the film.

In India, the numbers of theatres are increasing every day and the market of Bollywood films is constantly growing. A film is releasing simultaneously all over India with thousands of Digital prints. Therefore, the business of film is very important for the first 3 days as the numbers of people who can watch the movie on these days are becoming much larger. Therefore, it has become important to give necessary information about the movie to the audience so that movie can get good opening at the box-office.

From an actor's point of view, Marketing of movies is also very much essential. What an actor needs is just a lot of people watching him on screen. He wants many people to have access to his film. He wants his work to be seen by as many people as possible. He works very hard for a film and tries to bring different kind of things in it. If there is no audience, an actor is dead.

Hollywood has been following this process of movie marketing from a very long time. They are fantastic in marketing movies. They seem to have finest marketing brains. They spend a lot of money on that. Their marketing budget is 30-40% of their film budget. Movie marketing, in India, is at its nascent stage. "It's good for the industry that they have finally realized the importance of marketing and are innovating. Whether you are selling a movie or a 'bhelpuri', you need to have proper marketing," Alyque Padamsee mentioned once.

Pioneer of Movie-Marketing

Shahrukh Khan, the badshah of Bollywood, signifies the word 'Marketing. In Modern Indian Cinema, he has created new dimensions in Film-marketing. He has earned himself a reputation when it comes to movie promotions and marketing strategies. He is known for his suave marketing skills. He intends to go an extra mile when it comes to market movies. No one knows better than Shahrukh Khan that how to market an idea. He sells products. He is the face of many Indian as well as International brands and gets lot of money for doing that. He applies it to the film marketing. He does not mind endorsing his own films. He promotes them aggressively because he knows that if he is not aggressive; his movies will never exist in the minds of the audience. In addition, he has a set of people who know how to market a film. They know how to take it forward.

Bollywood Superstar Shahrukh Khan is the pioneer of trying to market movies in a different way. The actor strongly believes that he was the one who initiated this revolution in India with the movie *Yes boss* (1997). He shot a special trailer for the movie. With the movie *Phir bhi dil hai Hindustani* (2000), He had taken movie marketing to a completely new level. He shot a special promotional song just to market the movie. The song was not present in the movie but it was saying a lot of thing about the movie. In addition, being the producer of the film, he went to various cities to promote the movie and interacted with the distributors.

The movie released at a time when multiplexes had not come in India. At that time, nobody used to shot special promotional songs for movies. With this attempt, he shocked everyone. Although, he had copied it from the western cinema but at least, In India, he was the first one to start it. Now, everyone does it. Everybody is now following his footsteps. Therefore, in the true sense, he taught marketing to the Indian film Industry.

SRK's Marketing Style

Over the years, it is very common seeing film stars to do several promotional stunts in order to create hype about their movies but there is a different category of Shahrukh Khan. He understands the power of Marketing. He has its style of marketing movies. There is a class in the way he markets his movies. He never does any publicity drama or stunt before the release of his movies. He works by his own standards. He does all by different promotional methods and strategies. He is known for employing innovative marketing concepts to promote movies. He is known for creating buzz about his movies before its release through these marketing strategies. He is willing to do more maverick and dramatic things to promote them.

He works equally hard during the marketing of movies as he does while making the movie. He brings rare enthusiasm to his work and has an intuitive sense of marketing. In addition, the actor has a global appeal and his stardom works for him. He knows how to utilize his stardom to market his movies.

The Entertainment industry, in India, is very close to the world of Media. It makes a huge difference to the Indian cinema. It is powerful, impressionable and brings a lot of accountability. Bollywood actor Shahrukh Khan is quite aware of power of vibrant media these days. Being a media personality, he depends a lot on them. He is noted for being courteous and friendly with them. It is a huge Marketing asset. He is not savvy about Media. He respects them. His other qualities like knowledge, shrewd media handling and contemporary style of speaking in interviews also helps him to market his movies in a more efficient way because marketing, to a large extent, is about what to say and how to say it.

Shahrukh Khan believes that each film has a life of its own. Therefore, it has its own marketing strategy to inform the different target audience. It has a marketing base of its own. Only money should not be the criteria for marketing movies. According to him, Marketing of a film has nothing to do with getting extra eyeballs or tickets. It is the way to inform the audience only about the new things in the movie. He has good ideas about going out and telling people to watch a film depending upon the kind of film it is. During the release of *Chakde! India* (2007), he did not talk about the movie. It was a small budget movie with the kind of stardom attached to it. He is very proud of that movie. After the release of the movie, he did not give any interview about it. Even after the film got national award, he did not talk about it because the film was about young girls and empowerment of women in sports. They were the new factor in the movie and that was the simplicity and goodness of the movie. That was the whole idea. It was promoted in that way and it did well. People seem to like it.

During the promotions of *My Name is Khan* (2010), he went to different cities to find lovers with a unique love story because the film was a journey of Love. He went to cities like Ahmedabad, Lucknow, Indore, Delhi and Bangalore in search of that boy and girl, who had done something unique for Love. He did all through live stage performances.

Ra.one: Taking Film Marketing to a new Level

The Hindi film Industry's most charismatic actor Shahrukh Khan and his entire team in Red Chillies Entertainment went on a marketing blitzkrieg to promote his ambitious technological mega-venture *Ra.one*. They went all out to ensure that his movie get the opening that it deserves. The movie was a blockbuster entertainer. It was essentially a superhero film. It was about a character who comes out of a game. It was also a father-son story, which had the emotion and story. Besides being a superhero film, it also had never seen visual effects. That was the package, which they need to market. They pulled off some heroic marketing. The film was made with India's biggest stars, some of the world's best technical crew and with loads of visual effects. He attempted the promotion of the film on a big scale. It had changed the face of movie marketing in India. In addition, it received several awards for its marketing.

It was the Bollywood's most advertised film at the time of release. It was a different kind of film. The superhero genre was not much exploited in the country. The protagonist was in a different costume and look. It was unique in its approach. Therefore, the film needed a lot of telling and explaining.

Earlier, movie marketing was mainly done by putting up posters or letting everyone aware about the film by interviews. In this case, marketing was done through different areas of people's interest like video games and merchandising. Doing city tours, attending press conferences and giving interviews, Shahrukh Khan did all to promote it. The film introduced several means of Internet marketing. The promotions was done on all possible Digital and social media platforms. The actor has always believed that marketing should be informing to the audience about new things in the movie. From Digital world to gaming aspects, there were so many new things in the movie that he needed a lot more platforms to market it. The primary incentive is the incredible reach and an unprecedented level of scale that these medium provide.

Shahrukh Khan started the marketing of Ra.one in January 2011 by releasing the first look of the film on his twitter page. It was the first time in India that somebody attempted the marketing of a film nine months before the film was due for release.

In March, ten second trailer of the film was released on ESPN Star Sports during ICC Cricket World cup 2011 Quarter final match between India and Australia.

The first Theatrical trailer of Shahrukh Khan's dream project Ra.one was released three months later.

In September 2011, the music launch of the film took place. This was the biggest ever music launch of a Hindi film. The entire media covered it and it was telecasted on a TV channel.

Later, Shahrukh Khan's Red Chillies Entertainment team launched viral Marketing Campaign for promoting the film more effectively in the online arena. An official website of the movie was launched. An official custom-built 'Ra.one' channel was launched on YouTube, the first ever for an Indian film. The movie channel offered all promotional Video Content of the film. The actor was among one of the first Bollywood star to be on Google plus platform. He engaged with fans through live video chats and that was the big boost for the Networking site too.

Red Chillies Entertainment had a tremendous innovation through games to promote Ra.one. They had a tie-up with the Sony Computer Entertainment Europe to design a Ra.one game for the play station platform. UTV India games designed a Social game based on the film. Social games are the great tool to make marketing very entertaining and interesting in digital space. The attempt was to entice people especially young people who loves games. In a way, he made the marketing of the movie very interesting. The information about the movie went out to the audience in a most entertaining way. Therefore, it serves the dual purpose of Marketing as well as Entertainment.

'Ra.one' marketing was also driven through 'Barter System'. Shahrukh Khan opened the mind to it and collaborated with several brands to promote the film and their merchandise. It was a symbiotic marketing, which had never done in India. He did not spend so much money in the marketing as compared to the making of the film. Most of the film budget was spent on Production. A small portion was spent on the film marketing. It was mainly done with number of tie-ups and a big level of merchandising as well. From creating expensive film merchandising to getting some of Shahrukh Khan's existing brand endorsements as well as new brands on board, a complex partnership had been forged to keep *Ra.one* top of the mind. The association of the film with very well-known and trusted brands like Nokia, Nerolac, Videocon, Google, Sony Play Station, Godrej consumer products, Coco-Cola, Gitanjali group, Horlicks, Western Union, McDonalds helped to take the marketing forward. All the brands ensured that their association would produce strategic benefits.

It was a different kind of film. There was a new concept in the movie. Therefore, all the brands helped to market the movie in a way that people get the right information about the movie.

The marketing tie-ups had substantially funded the entire marketing budget of the film and produced strategic benefits. With merchandising, they tried to put everything on the market as cheap as possible and hoped that surrogate marketing for the film. In addition, the actor lent his image, time and name in return for Ra.one based media Campaigns and activations.

A glimpse of villain Ra.one character was disclosed couple of weeks before the film released.

Shahrukh Khan had appeared in three different TV shows 'India's got talent', 'Sa Re Ga Ma lil champs' and 'Just Dance' Simultaneously. He also returned to 'Kaun Banega Crorepati' as a guest to promote the movie.

Ra.one was also associated with Sahara Force India Formula 1 team. After the film released, the film's logo appeared right up in the front of the F1 car at India's first ever Formula one event.

The extensive marketing campaign of the movie were described as the "most comprehensive and all pervasive among people's lives." According to media analysts, Another unique aspect for Ra.one marketing campaign was that it was a case of integrating a film into every aspect of people's live, For instance, Clothing, automobiles, games, sports and merchandising.

KKR Promotional Activities

Shahrukh Khan is someone who really believes in professionalizing sports in India. He has passion for sports. He has been a keen sportsman since his school days. He wanted to prove himself in the sports arena too so he went all out for the promotions of his IPL team- Kolkata Knight riders. No other team was promoted the way KKR was. He is the marketer of his own businesses. Rather than hiring other film stars or giving stakes to other film star to promote them, Shahrukh Khan understands that he is a brand that can leverage to promote his own team, products or initiatives.

In 2008, when Kolkata Knight Riders were introduced, the logo of the team consisted of blazing golden Viking helmet against a black background with the name of the team Kolkata Knight

Riders written in gold and the tagline was "All the king's Men." The colors of team were Black and Gold during the first two seasons of IPL. None of the things that happened in Kolkata Knight Riders was done by fashion. They were done by the ideologies. The ideology is power. He truly believes that black is the color of *Kali maa*(Hindu Goddess) in Kolkata which stands for power, speed and wanting to vanquish demons from the face of the earth. Thus, the black was for that. Actor Shahrukh Khan wants every children to know that there is no problem in wanting to desire more in life. God has given life so that you work hard honestly and achieve whatever you want. There is no point in winning the silver. You just lose the Gold. What they have to do is to go for the victory. It is always golden in color. Thus, the ideology of the team was you go for the gold and do it with power. Later, it was changed to Purple and Gold.

The whole concept of golden helmet was introduced. It was the object of desire if you really believe that you can work very hard towards your goals. So if you only deserve it, desire it otherwise you cannot own a golden helmet.

In addition, a music video for the theme song of the team featuring Shahrukh Khan was released as part of the promotion. The theme song was *Korbo, Lorbo, Jeetbo Re* (We will do it, fight for it and win it). The whole ideology about the song was that how one should live life by these three words. Life is about doing, fighting and winning. During IPL2, another music video for the song called "Too Hot, Too cool" was filmed in which Khan took part. Despite of many failures, Shahrukh Khan did not stop the promotional activities for his team. In 2012, a new marketing Campaign was launched namely "New Dawn New Knights" to refresh the teams brand identity. The Logo of the team was replaced by blazing purple Corinthian helmet.

Shahrukh Khan is very successful in thinking up interesting marketing connections. Red Chillies TVC division handles some brands that he endorses, which is a very smart marketing fit. Similarly, for Kolkata Knight Riders, he used some of the brands that he represents like Nokia. A number of corporate sponsorships associated themselves with Khan-owned franchise. Over the years, they have sponsorship deals with Sansui, Seiko, Royal stag, Gitanjali Group, Star Plus, Dish TV, Rose valley, U.S. Polo Assn.,

The Telegraph, Fever 104 FM, SAP AG and Amazon.in among several others. Some apparel Sponsors of the team were Nokia, Matrix, XXX energy drink, Rose Valley, U.S. Polo Assn. and Reebok. All these associations and partnerships helped him to pull Kolkata Knight Riders through IPL.

Shahrukh Khan uses different marketing tools to promote movies but the superstar refuses to be labelled as "Marketing guru." He does not take the tag too seriously. He absolutely hates it when people termed his passion for movies as marketing. He finds it very disturbing when people talk about marketing of his movies. He just wants the whole world to see his movies. "These terms are all nonsensical things. Every actor has to talk about his films. I have been talking about my film from so many years. In fact, I tried to bring new things with every film of mine, but I am no marketing guru," the actor told reporters on the sidelines of an event. He added "But I do feel in order to reach out to more people one needs to be innovative so that more and more people can be made aware about your film and that's what I am doing."

He believes that the first rule of communication or entertainment is to get enough people in the room to, at least, see the entertainment. The idea is to inform people what the film stands for. It is just a louder voice to tell people to watch his movies and the rest follows from there.

7
A human brand called SRK

The Inimitable and Indefatigable Shahrukh Khan started his career by appearing in several television serials in the late 1980s like *Dil-Dariya, fauji* and *Circus*. He had made a name for himself in Television. Now after becoming a huge Bollywood Superstar, he dominated the small screen as an ambassador for multiple brands. He has been endorsing innumerable products. Companies from all over the world use Shahrukh Khan to sell their products and services. As a brand endorser, he is very expensive. He charges a huge amount of money for a few days of work.

He is one of the most saleable faces of new-age India. He is a popular face of endorsements. He has mastered the art of selling products. He is the face that launches thousand products. He is on billboards and on television, endorsing beverages, paints, Interiors, Cars, watches, toothpaste and even a state. Like his films, each commercial is delight to watch. He is brilliant whether he is endorsing a brand or whether he simply plays an actor in the television commercial. Due to his various brand endorsements, the concept of brand SRK is quite popular in India. It is one of the biggest brands of the Bollywood firmament. It is a brand, which everyone relates. In the era of aspiration and materialism, several corporate sectors and top-notch multinational brands are ready to sink heavy money on brand SRK for print and television advertisements. It is an interesting case study for MBAs.

Branding is about connecting, and in some way engaging with people. Shahrukh Khan, one of the most recognized and idealized personality of the world definitely has huge influence over the audience. His connect with children, youth and women have made him probably the first choice to promote ideas and products. His popularity and stardom greatly helps in enhancing the brand image of the product. It helps to make a good perception about the product in the minds of consumer.

The actor is more accessible to public. He, in some way, connects better with the audience. He is the favorite among the media. He is quite aware of his stardom and market value. Only a few Indian actors can match up to Shahrukh Khan's market value in the sophisticated Indian market. He projects an aura of glamour. His success ratio, credibility and persona are totally unmatched. He has redefined stardom in modern times. His star value is undeniable and today his name is associated with values such as loyalty and trust. He does not hesitate to use it.

Shahrukh Khan has never tried to convert himself into a brand. He does what he does the best. According to him, a brand has to be at its simplest level. Sometime people find connotations and meanings out of him and he finds it wonderful that some meanings that he does not think of, he stands for it. People say he stands for love, romance and family values but the actor believes these things happen naturally. People gives him logo, sign or a name but he tries to keep it simple and straight.

Over the years, he has taken the world of advertising by storm. His mantra for brand creation is "Early to bed, early to rise, work like hell and advertise,"- a notable quote of American Entrepreneur Ted Turner.

Shahrukh Khan does endorsements because he wants to do films of choices of what story to tell. They have given him the freedom to do the kind of cinema that he wanted to do. He utilized those earnings to make bigger and better films. He respects and thanks all the products that he has endorsed over the years. If he did not make that money may be he would not be able to do Cinema that he wanted to do. "The endorsements I do allows me to make the films that I want to. There have been times when I fell short of money during Om Shanti Om, I went to all my companies, and I said Listen guys! I need 5-7 crore rupees to complete it. I don't want to sell the film. Can I do an ad Or Can you sign me on? They were like of course. Why not? They all have been very helpful," the actor said. It has worked for him. Therefore, he is extremely thankful to all the people who has taken him as an ambassador and paid him good amount of money.

Bollywood's leading man Shahrukh Khan is the face of several big products and brands producing by big corporates and companies. They take a big risk when they just take a face for what they have done for several years. They are putting their reputation on line. He respects that. Whatever the brand he endorses, he works with a sense of responsibility because several number of people work with those brands and huge amount of money is involved. "When you are a brand ambassador for anything, any of the products or even a leading man for a film or a producer, I think you have a lot of responsibility. Apart from the fact that we have fun, crack jokes and have a sense of humour, whatever I do, I do it with a sense of responsibility," he mentioned.

Shahrukh Khan, one of the biggest names of the Indian Cinema, have endorsed luxury TAG Heuer watches, Hindustan Unilever's Soap Lux, Belmonte suiting, Zee Network Enterprise's division Dish TV, Emami skincare brand, mayor suiting and ITC's Sunfeast. Some of the other products and brands which have endorsed by Shahrukh Khan over the years include Pepsi, Videocon, Airtel, HP, Sprite, Hyundai, Nerolac Paints, Nokia, Top Ramen curry smoodles, Linc Pen, Pepsodent, D'décor furnishing, Gitanjali jewels, Bagpiper whisky, VI- john, Navratna, Dabur Sona chandi and Compaq Presario amongst others. These big products come his way. He feels extremely proud to be associated with these brands.

Apart from endorsing corporate products, he has been associated with several governmental campaigns like Pulse Polio Immunization, National Aids Control Organization (NACO), National Rural Health Mission and Water Sanitation Hygiene (WASH). He has also been the brand ambassador of a sports league and an Indian state. In 2011, he was the face of the Champions League Twenty20. In 2012, he was appointed as the brand ambassador of the state of West-Bengal.

Shahrukh Khan has never worked to build a brand of his name. He never worked in any special manner to consciously build his brand. He does things exactly what he did when he joined the Indian Entertainment industry.

- He works very hard. The greatest quality that makes him a dynamic personality is his ability to work hard with complete devotion to achieve what he wants. That is the essence of his life. He gives suitable time to each brand he is associated.
- He tries to offer people what he is being paid for i.e. Entertainment at whatever cost.
- He tries to be very honest in his dealings with the audience for which he makes films.

These are the most conventional old-fashioned ways, which helps him to make a brand of his name. He has done exactly what most of the greatest brands have been able to do conventionally. Apart from this, he does not do anything to build it up further.

Celebrity Endorsements

Celebrity Endorsements is a globally recognized phenomenon. In this competitive environment, it considered as a winning formula by the corporate to market their products. Celebrities are special. They have higher glamour quotient and bigger appeal. They are perceived as God by their millions of fans. They are worshipped as idol. Consumers believe that they can enhance themselves by forming connections with the brand or product endorsed by celebrities. Everybody likes to associate with the person on screen. People like celebrities. If those celebrities say that they like a certain product or brand, people will like that too. Marketers use this connection for holding the attention of companies target customer. These celebrities are roped to make the product popular.

The association of a celebrity adds glamour, charm and aspiration to the product. They provide quick visibility and transfer values to a product or a company. They can change the perception of a brand and consequently increases revenue. In a way, they support company's belief.

In an emerging market like India, there is a high proliferation of Indian and international brands. In this highly competitive world, often these brands need a face that can extend his/her popularity and stature to the brands. Companies need big names to promote their brand and adding a face to a brand can be a key differentiating factor. Several small brands and SMEs have gained a lot from the celebrity Endorsements.

Bollywood actor Shahrukh Khan is the most preferred icon for celebrity endorsements in India. He fulfills all the requirements of celebrity Endorsements. He is a celebrity who is able to promote the significant characteristics of the product or brand. He stands for all the propriety and goodness that a company stands for. He has won the trust and confidence of millions of people across the world. Hailed to be the Numero Uno of Bollywood, Shahrukh Khan lends the factor of believability, integrity and honesty in his endorsements. His larger than life persona makes him favorite among the advertising world.

Shahrukh Khan is the ultimate king of the Indian Entertainment Industry. The actor strongly believes that he is one of the few Indian Celebrities who initiated this revolution in India. He was the first one who introduced the 'success formula' of Celebrity Endorsements. He started single handedly endorsements in Indian film Industry. Actors used to look down upon appearances in Endorsements. Nobody used to do before him. He changed that. "I side stepped a wee bit to become Shahrukh Khan the seller, from Shahrukh Khan the buyer. Celebrity endorsements are an old phenomenon, but in India, I like to believe I was one of the guys who started it all. Before my time, actors hardly advertise for products and at least not for lots of products," He said at the Ad Asia Conference 2011.

Shahrukh Khan believes that till then, it was thought that an actor loses enigma if he endorsed a product or brand. The enigmatic quality of an actor goes away with the advertised product.

"I was told an actor loses his enigma, his appeal if he sells product," Shahrukh Khan said.

He broke the myth that actors lose their enigma, appeal, wonder and become a commodity by getting into endorsements. He said that he was "too poor" to be a wonder and started endorsing brands as he believed that people like to associate with the actors they see on screen and that actually is a wonder. In addition, he likes the concept of image being link to a product. He finds it quite interesting to tell a story in 30 seconds. He respects that. For him, Silver screen is not the only way to connect with the audience. He enjoys working on small screen. He has no issues about the platform. He enjoys any platform where he can act. His efforts and entertainment values on that platform is important. He feels proud of doing that. Things have changed. Even now, stardom or star value is measured by the price of endorsements that an actor has.

TAG Heuer, the Swiss watch brand, entered India in 2002 and opted Bollywood superstar Shahrukh Khan as a brand ambassador to expand its presence. The actor relates to it. He is very proud to be associated with the brand. TAG Heuer has a long history with sports and cinema. Many celebrities have been a part of this luxury watchmaker family, making it a brand synonymous with sports and glamour in India as well as internationally.

In 2005, Shahrukh Khan became the first male superstar to endorse a woman's product in India. Hindustan Unilever roped Shahrukh Khan to endorse beauty soap Lux, a soap that had been endorsed by leading female actors only thus far. At that time, Lux was celebrating 75 years of stardom. In the commercial, the actor was shown immersed in a bathtub full of rose petals along with four leading ladies of Bollywood sitting outside. With this advertisement, he represented an image of a metrosexual man. It certainly created a buzz, as it was an unconventional and bold thing for India's biggest male star to do, not worried about his macho image. However, he finds it fun thing and nothing deeper than that.

In September 2011, Shahrukh Khan was chosen the brand ambassador for the 2011 edition of the Nokia champions League Twenty20. His team Kolkata Knight Riders was also in with a chance of qualifying for the main edition of the tournament. He felt extremely proud and blessed that he had given the opportunity to be associated with a sporting event. As a team owner, he felt very happy that he had given a chance to do something in the sports arena too.

In October 2011, Shahrukh Khan was named a global Ambassador by the WSSCC (World Supply Sanitation and Collaborative Council) Global Sanitation and Hygiene forum to advocate Water, Sanitation and Hygiene issues. He was, in fact, the first celebrity global ambassador on these issues. The WSSCC works to ensure sustainable sanitation, better hygiene and safe drinking water for the people all across the world.

In 2012, West Bengal Chief Minister Mamta Banerjee enlisted Bollywood star Shahrukh Khan as state's brand ambassador. In his reply, he accepted the offer with great humility. Shahrukh Khan shares a close intimacy with Bengal. His connection with Bengal is through his IPL cricket team Kolkata Knight Riders. He loves the state like anything. In Bengal, there is high level of interest in Cinema. There cannot be a marketer other than Shahrukh Khan for Bengal.

The actor is extremely proud of being the brand ambassador of the state. He took it with as much responsibility as he gives to anything else he does. He takes time to figure out what he can do for the state. He started it with a small film about the promotion of West-Bengal. In the video, he called the new Bengal a 'Progressive Bengal' and invited tourists and investors from across the globe to come and experience things that are special about the state. The promotional film highlighted various historic, cultural and industrial landmarks of West-Bengal with Shahrukh Khan saying, "The World is a beautiful place but there is something special about Bengal."

Brands and Ambassadors: 'Symbiotic relationship'

Shahrukh Khan is an obvious choice for brand endorsements. He gets many offers for promoting ideas and products and he does not mind selling anything but when it comes to cigarettes and tobacco, he does not endorse it because, in the larger context, these things are not good for the health of the people. He does not encourage that at all. He considers only those which he feels are right. He also believes that if people think it should advertised, it should be but if it is a wrong thing, then, no amount of advertising and stardom can help to promote the product. The quality speaks the volume.

Shahrukh Khan finds it unfair to expect from him to know everything about the products that he endorses. He believes that Ambassadors should have limited liability for the products they endorse as they only have limited knowledge about products. They should not be held completely accountable because there are agencies and checking points all around societies and in governmental organizations to check those products much before a star can check and verify them even better. If they over-look something, then how an ambassador can find out everything. The important thing for the brand ambassador is to be able to talk about the product properly. Therefore, whenever he is asked about the quality of the product or brand that he endorse, he always maintained, "They choose me, I don't choose them." He does not have any right, position or even intelligence to choose a brand. He has respect for everybody's brand. He never question any aspect of it. Therefore, when a brand comes to him, they honor him. They pay him very well. He owes a huge amount of alliance to them. He really believes that their product is the best. Therefore, if it is legal, the country is selling it and there is a tax on it, he does not mind endorsing them. It is a symbiotic relationship that brand and ambassador shares.

Secondly, he thinks that there are only good products that come his way. He has always been associated with products that have a lot of history behind them. He gets the products of greatest quality because of his status and recognition that he has achieved as an actor. He believes that these products or brands are great properties even if he is not endorsing them.

Performance leads Brands

In the world of Endorsements, there is a downside of branding. If a brand is not capable to deliver, it can finish. This often happens with celebrities and, increasingly, it is becoming challenging. A

Brand is a promise and un-kempt promise is of no value. Therefore, it must have sustained values delivered to customer.

There is an old saying that "Product is mortal and brand is immortal," but this is changing in today's modern era because Technology is shrinking time and space. In addition, there are number of sources of information. Therefore, Association of brands will be transient. Indian Cricketer Yuvraj Singh, in an advertisement, said, "Jab tak balla chal raha hai, thaat hai warna.... (As long as your bat does the talking, you are on the top of the world, otherwise....). This is applicable for Branding.

In this highly competitive world, a brand remain alive and stay ahead of competition by two successful ways. Firstly, the brand should be capable to deliver. Secondly, it should update himself with the new generation. Actor Shahrukh Khan quite knows the fact that an actor need to stay in demand and maintain high success rate in order to meet the expectation of the people.

8

Commerce and Creativity

Money Matters

Shahrukh Khan has never denied his Love for fame and money. He does not mind to imagine good material things that he wants. "I was very clear that anything that is peripheral or an off-shoot of me becoming an actor or star, I will utilize to earn money from it," he said.

Shahrukh Khan is very open about telling youngsters that there is no problem in desiring a lot as long as you deserve it. He believes that in a material world, it is all right to have a certain amount of material comfort. According to him, material happiness is quite an important step before you look for spiritual happiness. It is a world where a certain level of consumerism has come to be a reality.

Shahrukh Khan feels that it is important to be economically well to do because if one is not economically stable, then he would not be able to make right choices. Lack of money always pushes down. It is important for one to make the choices that he wants to make. "I want people to be rich. I want people to be famous. I want people to do well in their life. I want them to feel once all the goodness and good things of life. They don't like it, they don't need to use it but they need to be having access to it. They should have the choice," the actor said. He has reached a level where money does not matter for him. He is in a position where he can afford to do anything but when he started his career, that time his dream was to have a house, car and everything. He hopes to God that everybody gets enough money so that it stops mattering for him or her.

Shahrukh Khan makes special appearances and dances at high profile weddings. He is highly priced for things like this. He has no qualms in admitting that he does all to earn money. He found nothing wrong in it. He believes that the happiest occasion for anyone is marriage and he loves to participate for him or her.

The actor does not charge money for attending a party or wedding. If somebody invites him for attending a party, he goes and attend it. However, if they want him to perform, then it becomes a show. He takes money for performing at the venue close to the wedding. It is a full stage like a live stage show. It is very expensive because he performs with large numbers of dancers. It is like shooting a huge Hindi song. That is why, it is expensive and unaffordable for many. He performs at the venue. The show starts at time. All the wedding guests come and attend it like a stage show.

Shahrukh Khan has a huge dignity of labour. He has no problem doing anything. He can act and dance anywhere. Wherever he gets a chance to perform, he does with dignity and exposes his full talent but money is always attached to it because he uses that money to create some great cinema in India so that he does not have to borrow money and worry about movie making.

"Nothing wrong in wanting to be rich, there is nothing in being ambitious and you don't have to justify yourself, you don't have to lie for it...as long as you know that you are right. You want to live in Taj Mahal, go ahead and live in Taj Mahal. You want a big car, work for it honestly, get it, drive it and be happy about it. Then, show off be arrogant be pompous and that's the way to be," he explained, "I don't think there is anything wrong if you have done it honestly, you have not cheated anyone. It's your money, it's your job, it's your passion and it's your love. And it's honest and hard work. Nothing can take that away from you. So when you say are you greedy? Yes! I am greedy. When you say you dance at weddings? Yes! I am proud of it because I am very clear. I want all these. I want these for my children, for my wife and for myself. The whole point is I want a life which I live on my terms."

Shahrukh Khan believes that money is a good thing to run after. It is very important to be financially stable but you have to keep your wrongs and rights in mind. Do not shy away from earning but without selling your soul. Addressing to people, he said, "I want to tell all the youngsters please do whatever you want to do in terms of being well-off materially but somewhere keep a spiritual thought that the world should be a better place because you are born in it."

When asked which is more important between work and money? He said, "I can safely say the type of work that brings a lot of money. That is the best. If that can't happen then... actually I always quote a saying in jest, never seriously till now, which goes... "Do your work and don't look for the fruits of your labour." I think at the end of it all money is not everything in life but it makes life one hell of easier place to be in if you have lot of money. So both ways it is... I really can't decide. I am greedy also so I go for money also and I go for work also. I work very hard and I want my pound of flesh also for that work."

Shahrukh Khan sells himself for endorsements and weddings but he does not charge anything to act in a film. In spite of all the trappings of commercial cinema, he never does the business of acting. The actor remembers the basic truth that an actor becomes a star because of the movies. Movies do not become great because of the stars. Therefore, he never has an expectation in terms of the business of film. He never does movies for money because making movies is life for him. Films are the cause of his existence and that is something he loves the most. He sign-up a film because of the story and people working in it. He does not have a price for a film. He does not discuss money for a film at all. In his words, "I started feeling that once I took moneys for a film without knowing what the film is; somehow I was obliged to start liking what those people were making." Therefore, he is priceless in that way. He knows very well that what he can control is the economics of the film. Thus, he never put a burden on the producer. He keeps it viable by making a fantastically expensive movie but he tries to utilize that money on the film expense, rather than utilizing on the star expense.

When a producer works with Shahrukh Khan, he does not worry about the price. The actor has been ambitious towards movie making. Acting in movies is his mainstay. Apart from making films, everything that he does is to put it into the films to make it better in terms of style and technology so that it appeals to the global audience.

In a sense, he has much more money that he needs to live a regular life but he has very little money considering what he wants to do. He wants to make a fantastic VFX film, which is never seen before. He wants to make a beautiful and technologically advanced film studio where he can make films of international standards. He has a number of dreams like this. For that, he has no money.

An Entrepreneurial genius

Bollywood Superstar Shahrukh Khan has found a place in billions of hearts, not only with his work in cinema but he has also made an indelible mark with his entrepreneurial genius. He has a very acute business acumen. He is an excellent entrepreneur and a true leader. In 2011, he has been presented with the Creative Entrepreneur of the year Award at NDTV profit's Business Leadership Awards. Apart from being an actor, he tries hands in several other things, which provide thrust to his businesses. In terms of wealth, he is richer than any other Bollywood contemporary. There are number of causes to which he feels doing passionately. He plans his moves carefully for maximum effectiveness and advantage. Business school students can learn a lot from Shahrukh Khan's style of doing business. People from very big business organization call him to give lecture on success and making an organization works. The sprawling business empire of Shahrukh Khan includes co-ownership of the glamorous Indian Premiere league cricket team Kolkata knight riders, Red Chillies Production, Shares in kidzania Mumbai, Brand endorsements, shows, events and dancing at weddings.

Asked about his core business philosophy, Shahrukh Khan said, "When things go right, everything goes right. My basic philosophy is very retail like *Subah ko dukan kholo, raat ko shutter down karo*(Open the shop in the morning, close it at night). I have seen people like Mukesh bhai (Mukesh Ambani) and Lakshmi Saab (Lakshmi Mittal). I have sat at their meetings and tried to understand what they say and do. They are awesome. I am nowhere close to them. For me, *bijli paani ka kharcha nikal jaaye* (if I am able to pay electricity and other bills, I am happy). That is how you start business."

Shahrukh Khan is a resilient. He failed in every business, which he started. He failed as a producer. He believes that there is a gestation period in every business and if a person is able to undergo that gestation period, then he became successful. If you stick on a business for long enough, it will grow. Success always comes after struggle. One needs to keep on trying.

Producer

Shahrukh Khan's main motivation is to do something creative and, most importantly entertaining. He couples commerce and creativity very well, which is the basic root of all his business ventures. By the end of 1990s, he got involved in producing films. He turned producer because he wanted to do creative stuff from the parallel side. He wanted to experiment as a producer. He has always wanted to make a different kind of film. He felt that if he believed in a particular kind of cinema, he should fund it. Under his production house, he produced films which nobody wanted to produce either they were too expensive or too offbeat. He has made films by signing other actor as a lead under his own production house.

In 1999, Shahrukh Khan started Dreamz unlimited with Juhi Chawla and Aziz Mirza. The experience of Dreamz unlimited taught some important lessons to Shahrukh Khan. The company produced four films. *Phir bhi dil hai Hindustani*(2000), the first production venture of the company, was about the commercialization of media with a real message but the film did not do well. From being a superstar, suddenly, he was told that he is not good enough as an actor. His production is not good enough. People started writing on tabloids and magazines that he is finished as an actor. His movie career is over. He was compared with the newcomers, which was quite embarrassing and sad. He got very depressed. It was one of the most depressing phase of his filmy Career.

After this, Shahrukh Khan acted and produced the beautiful shot *Asoka*(2001) - a film based on one of India's greatest Emperor Asoka. While the movie was critically acclaimed and Shahrukh's performance was praised, the movie failed to create any magic at the box-office.

One 2 ka 4 (2001) was the third movie of dreamz unlimited. In spite of its impressive star cast, the film was flopped at the box office. Dreamz unlimited did not seem such a promising venture anymore.

Chalte-Chalte (2003) was the last production of Dreamz unlimited. The movie was a hit but after this release, Shahrukh Khan took over the company and reformed it as Red Chillies Entertainment.

Red Chillies Entertainment

Shahrukh Khan's partner, this time, was his own partner in life, Gauri Khan. His determination and never say die attitude brought Red Chillies Entertainment a huge success. His production company has given chances to small budget films where new and fresh stories can become movies. In a way, he has given small films a big reach. The movies produced by Red Chillies Entertainment have won several awards. The production company is a major part of his life, which allows him to make films, which he likes and gives him artistic freedom.

The first venture of the new production house was Farah Khan's directorial debut film *Main hoon na* (2004), in which Shahrukh Khan starred as well. With Shahrukh Khan's company behind the project and his face in front of the camera, the movie was a commercial success and was among the highest grossing film of the year. The success of *Main hoon na* brought a steadiness to the Red Chillies production.

In 2005, Shahrukh Khan starred in lavish looking *Paheli,* which was company's second film. It was a risk. The film's story was presented in a beautiful way. Shahrukh Khan's look also changed with the role. Along with having a different story and big cast, the film was more offbeat than mainstream. The movie did not leave its mark at the box office but critics praised the film and it was selected as India's official entry to the 79th Academy Awards in the best foreign language film category.

In the same year, the company co-produced the horror film *Kaal,* in which there was a number of great actors. Khan also performed an item number for the film. The film did moderately well at the box office.

In 2007, Khan was appeared in *Om Shanti Om,* which was a dramatic, humorous and a big scale reincarnation film. It was a highly celebrated film, which brought some elements of 1970s. The director had taken the backdrops of cinema of that era and tried to tell a story. The film was a blockbuster and the most successful film of the year. It also emerged as one of the biggest hit of Shahrukh Khan's career.

In 2009, the company produced *Billu,* which was about stories of two friends. There has two different world meeting with each other. It was a story of an ordinary person in a small town; a movie star came into the town and how things changed. The movie was about meeting of two different cultures. One was real with small little problems of life while the other was very unreal that look very glamorous and happy from outside. Shahrukh Khan played a supporting role in the movie. He played the character as a pre-conceived notion of a movie star. The movie was praised for its simple storytelling and was declared a 'semi-hit' at the box-office.

In 2010, Red Chillies entertainment co-produced *my name is Khan.* It was about a universal truth that the world become paranoid of each other. People are grouping each other by action of few. The film reunited actor Shahrukh Khan and his frequent onscreen pair Kajol who played his wife in the movie. They played a very challenging role of their career in the movie. Rizwan Khan, an honorable man from India living with Asperger syndrome fall in love with Mandira, played by Indian actress Kajol- a Hindu single mother. Then, the 9/11 incident happened and it affected their life incidentally. The film was about how 9/11 affected their life and how the love just completely disrupted. The film was set against the real life incident of 9/11 but that incident is not the mainstay of the movie. It was garbed under a love story and there was a message of humanity. They addressed the issues between Islam and the western world on a humanitarian level rather than addressing it on a political level. The movie mostly received positive reviews and done very well, both in India as well as across the world.

In 2011, the company produced the path breaking Bollywood movie 'Ra.one.' The movie was one its kind as the superhero genre was reflected in the movie. It opened strongly at the box office but some critics noted weak in terms of its storytelling.

In 2012, Red Chillies Entertainment co-produced Student of the Year. The movie received mixed reviews from critics and gained good collection at the box office.

In 2013, Red Chillies Entertainment produced the action romantic comedy film *Chennai Express*. It was a story of a north Indian man who fall in love with a south Indian girl and how true love conquered all cultural and language barrier. The movie smashed the box office records. It was declared as the mega blockbuster hit at the box office.

After the runaway success of *Chennai Express,* the company produced highly celebrated *Happy new year* (2014). The movie introduces a bunch of losers. They coincidentally encounter and make a master plan of robbing a bank in Dubai but to accomplish this mission, they need to participate in a dance competition. With Shahrukh Khan's company behind the project and his face in front of the camera, the film was an instant hit at the box office.

Red Chillies Entertainment has come a long way since its inception and rendered meaningful services to the Indian film Industry. Over the years, it has grown in terms of marketing, technology and presenting the film. They have wonderful set of people who learn on the field while making films. They have always tried new things. They have made small films like *Paheli* (2005) and big films like *Ra.one* (2011). They do some amazing things like Visual effects and technology that they use in various sequences that are as good as any International film can show. They learn it. What they learn in the last film, they try to make it perfect in the next one. In addition, it has attempted to create a little more cinematic value in Television.

As an enterprise, Red Chillies Entertainment has more flexibility to run faster. It continues to grow at a healthy pace in the global entertainment portal. It has interest in every field of entertainment possible. While films remain their flagship business, it has diversified its business greatly. Red Chillies VFX, a sub division of Red Chillies Entertainment, is offering platform as the state of the art visual effect provider for feature films and commercials. It is an operated post-production studio specializing in stunning visual effects. Over the years, the company has done quality visual effects in films like *Main hoon na* (2004), *Paheli* (2005), *Don* (2006), *Om Shanti Om* (2007), *What's your Raashee* (2009), *Ra.one* (2011), *Krrish3* (2013), *Chennai Express* (2013) and *Happy new year* (2014).

The Indian filmmakers are now becoming aware of the potential of visual effects, not from the creative point of view but also from the cost and production point of view. Eventually, films, stories and projects are coming where visual effects are a center point. There are reasons which driven the growth of Visual effects in the Indian film industry. It can save time and cost. It can cut down the risk factor. It can also fix something that can go wrong during the film shoot.

Shahrukh Khan believes that apart from the technology, the next big thing in Indian cinema would be visual effects. "Mr. Will Smith met me once and he told me that he does two films a year. One that is artistic for him as an actor and the second one with a bigger superstar than him as a co-star. When I asked him who would that be... he said visual effects. I feel so odd that on one hand we have the biggest software developing industries of the world happening in our cities and our country and somehow we are so lagging behind in its usage in India," he said. A visual effect, In India, are in its infancy and has a great scope in Indian popular cinema.

In his small way, Shahrukh Khan's biggest dream in life has always been to try and make an International class studio for the country, not for profit or any other reason but for the fact that India can make better films, which the whole world can watch. He wants to make something that enhances the filmmaking in India. His vision is to create a platform where other Indian filmmakers, directors, writers and storytellers can utilize the technology to tell bigger, better and more beautiful stories. He believes that a good Studio, a good Sound stage and a good postproduction unit will always enhances the film. With the production house, he wants to make typical Indian film, which the whole world embraces. That will be stunning for the Indian cinema. India has a huge market. The numbers of International studios are coming in India. The actor wants to create entertainment infrastructure in India. He wants to give infrastructure to the world. He wants International filmmakers to come to India and use their resources. He wants to give platform and enough space to the Indian as well as the world cinema to grow further.

Shahrukh Khan honestly believes that in life, nobody attains everything individually. It has to be team effort. He has always been a team player. He likes to work in a team whether it is a filmmaking or business. Over the years, he has collected a set of creative people who knows how to make a film and he wants to give wings to them. Most of his businesses prosper because hardworking, smart and intelligent people who work in Red Chillies Entertainment always surround him. They are dedicated to the purpose of the company. More than being great business managers, these people understand what he wants and they have taken his talent and hard work beyond what he deserves. "As a matter of fact, I think I am what I am because of the team that has surrounded me. People just give me the name because my face is on the posters but if I didn't have a good team of people working and making me who I am I would be nobody," he said.

Shahrukh Khan has never borrowed money. He likes to have ownership over things, which are material. He does not like to lease, rent or borrow. He likes to own them. Therefore, if he is having a cricket team, he does not want to be brand ambassador of the team. He wants to own the team. He wants to be the heart of it rather than being the face of it. Everything that is invested in the Company is completely personal. That is what they have tried to maintain. The money is essentially brought in personally and then being earned back as years has gone. Therefore, it is debt-free.

Kolkata Knight Riders

The Indian Premier League (IPL) is the richest and the most popular Cricket tournament in the world. It is a form of cricket and has a huge amount of entertainment value. It is a clear crowd pleaser. It creates a different form of spectator buzz. It caught the imagination of the world because it is interesting, stylish and glamorous. It became an event due to the presence of actors and other glamorous people. The IPL experience is something, which the Indian viewer had not felt before.

In 2008, Kolkata knight riders- a franchise representing Kolkata in the Indian Premier League was owned by super wealthy actor Shahrukh Khan's Red Chillies Entertainment in partnership with actress Juhi Chawla and her husband Jay Mehta for USD 75.09 Million (₹ 357 Crores). Buying a cricket franchise in the Indian Premier League was a huge risk.

Shahrukh Khan is a risk taker. Lot of the risk, which he took are fairly calculated risk. From business point of view, he does not enter in any business venture without knowing what the outcome would be. He must have had careful assessment of what the result would be. For him, it is important to try something new and different, even if it meant putting his name and money at stake.

Shahrukh Khan has redefined himself as one of the most powerful man in India when he bought an IPL Cricket team. He is a mentor and felicitator of a side, which he built from a scratch. He did not go ahead to marry Bollywood and Cricket. He did not buy the IPL team as a movie star. He had bought the team as an individual who loves sports. There was an interest, which he had. He just happened to be a movie star. It is an individual choice. It is not necessarily follows that every movie star would have the same vision. The only selling aspect of the IPL is Cricket and the actor truly believes that if the Cricket is not good, then nobody would come to watch it. The IPL exists because of the quality of Cricket that is being played. In addition, there has been business opportunities in the IPL. It has been a great business Model. It receives most of the money from variety of means like television rights, franchise rights and sponsors. Franchisees also receives money from different ways like Stadium Cricket sales, advertising, merchandising, sponsorship and earnings from Central revenue.

The business model for IPL is a difficult model. Shahrukh Khan need to take some risk and he need to have patience, as the team does not win, the business aspect of the team starts falling down. He just being a movie star cannot lead it. It is an aspect of cricketing model that IPL follows.

Apart from the business opportunities, he had a different vision for buying an IPL Cricket team. Shahrukh Khan's company is not a Public limited company. They have limited resources. They have the nicest run as far as the economics of the team concerned but he never equated his team to make money. For him, Buying a cricket team is not a losing proposition as a business but he has not gone into cricket for the business. He loves sports. He felt disappointed when his team lost matches. In addition, he had the vision that he always wanted to do something for sports in his own small way. He wanted to create a professional platform for sports in India because according to him, it is important for Indians to be interested in sports. He wanted to set up an area where younger people have an option to become Professional sportsman, if not internationally or nationally at least domestically, earn money and follow their passion. He likes youngsters to do that in the country.

Shahrukh Khan's involvement in the team was limited only to the entertainment part of it. The whole set of technical teams were headed by the experts. The cricketing aspect was left to the cricket experts. The idea of twenty-twenty cricket is to invoke a sense of speed and aggression. It gets over in 20 overs so there is a need of a focus team. The team selection was left mostly to the experts. He did not participate in it because his knowledge about cricket is limited.

Kidzania

Kidzania- the only place in the world where children can think, play, work and feel like an adult. It is a brand in the children Entertainment business. It is an ultimate indoor theme park, which recreates an incredibly realistic urban landscape with streets, shops, theatre and buildings. It allows children to work in adult jobs and earn currency by performing tasks in various activities.

Dedicated to corporate social responsibilities, Kidzania is designed to make children think about things on a much bigger scale. It teaches about the various roles playing options that a child can have. A child learns about social empowerment, social responsibilities and learns to be a good citizen. It compliments education rather than replacing it.

This is one of the most exciting thing for Bollywood actor Shahrukh Khan. He owns some shares in Kidzania Mumbai but it is not a business for him. It is not something, which he thought of as a venture. It is a heart-felt desire to do something for children in the country. Among his various business ventures, this is closest to his heart because all his life, everything he has learned and everything that he does, is always being for children. He finds nothing more entertaining and enriching than children.

Shahrukh Khan believes that Kidzania is one of the finest mixes of entertainment and education. It is a concept of empowering, educating and entertaining children. It enables them to figure out about the new world that they would face and actually be the creator of that new world. It is an attempt to bring the concept of socialization, which is an important aspect of children growing up.

Television Presenter

Shahrukh Khan has worked in television before making a transition to films after which he has never looked back. Television has made Shahrukh Khan a household name and he always acknowledges that. He always wants to works on television. He feels important to do it because he wants to give back to television what television has given to him. Hence, in 2007, he came back to television with the popular quiz show *Kaun Banega Crorepati*: India's franchised version of *who wants to be a millionaire*. He presented the show in his own style and sense of humor. The show found the new audience. It was very successful particularly with women and young people. He lived up to the expectations of the people and did very successfully.

In 2008, he hosted the quiz show *kya aap paanchvi paas se tez hain*, the Indian version of "Are you smarter than a 5th grader." It was a children-oriented program, which was very difficult for the contestants actually.

In 2011, he presented the Show *Zor ka jhatka: Total wipeout,* the Indian version of American show *Wipeout*. It was very different show as compared to Khan's earlier shows but, at the same time, was very funny.

In 2015, Superstar Shahrukh Khan returned to small screen and anchored quiz game show *India Poochega- Sabse shaana kaun.* It was very lively and fun show for the family. It had a far-reaching effect for the common person. For Shahrukh Khan, it was a normal show because it was related to his personality. He comes from a background of a common person. He understands their worries.

In India, not all actors are good anchors. There are many things, which works for Shahrukh Khan. He has a very quick, sharp wit and a sense of humor, which works very well on the shows. He is a sporting person. He enjoys playing games and wants to win it. In addition, he is one of the most charismatic star. His charisma and style works very well on these game shows.

In addition to his appearances as a Television presenter, he participates in several award shows as a host or stage performer. He is a true professional when it comes to hosting an award show.

Given his popularity around the world, he participates in several world tours and concerts, entertaining his millions of fans around the world.

People say that Shahrukh Khan is truly a man with Midas touch. He has been made to believe by the world that whatever he does turns out well. All his businesses proves that whatever he touches turns profitable, if not immediately then eventually.

Customer is King

Shahrukh Khan was an Economic student but he has a basic large-hearted understanding of business. His has an interest in business, which is beyond profits. He follows the most conventional age-old business mantra- Customer is King. According to him, the idea of a business should be at a level, which totally satisfies and delights the end user. It should be in the interest of consumer rather than any narrow economic objective. It should always be that the final consumer should be happy. It should be able to change or touch the lives of the end user. If the end user is satisfied, then sky is the limit as far as business is concerned. The business should be done that way.

The main objective of Shahrukh Khan's business ventures is to spread happiness. The purpose of business is not to sustain it. It should touch people and make them feel for that moment. This is the essential aspect of business that he knows. "Business is an idea and the idea of the business should always be that the consumer you are servicing, you should change his or her life," he said in a candid interview with renowned trade analyst Komal Nahta.

Creativity

Sometime People, who are devoted to art and passionate about creativity, selects a non-creative path due to certain practical realities of Life. They choose safer, more traditional non-creative path in life because they feel that the creative path is too risky, no matter how brave they are. However, Shahrukh Khan is a creative person. He breathes the air of Creativity. He combines a creative mind with high passion and quest for excellence. For him perfection is not a goal. He truly believes that the struggle or yearning for perfection is a wrong struggle. Life should have some imperfections. Beauty lies in having some non-beautiful things.

He is extremely passionate about creativity. Anything new or creative arouses his interest. He has the desire to create new things in the work field that he has. He is an institution in himself when it comes to creativity. The world has experienced Shahrukh Khan through his Creative expressions, which comes from the deepest experiences of Life. He emphasizes new values, new opportunities and new Ideas. "I do lot of advertising. Lot of people question me on the uncreative bits of work that I do. I think out of 10 things that

I do, seven of them are highly uncreative and very disturbing at times. I have a big bathroom now, I sit there and cry after having done those things [Laughs]," he said by adding "But I take the money from that and I would like to be able to create a production house, a filmmaking institution, which would do the creative stuff which I wanted to do when I was 25."

Sharing his views on Creativity, Bollywood star Shahrukh Khan said, "See the full result. Did the whole thing make a good effect? If you work for the whole, you will somewhere down the line succeed more often than not. If you work for parts, you will be partly successful. If you work for the whole, you will be wholly successful."

Shahrukh Khan believes that money, fame, lovely car and big house are peripherals of work. These things are not core of existence and work. These things are never supposed to be what he set out in life. The core is he needs to do his work with honesty and hard work. The core is that he is a creative person. He set out for being a creative person and due to his creativity, he is getting money, fame, goodness, sadness, respect and praise. In addition, he is quite aware of the fact that if he cannot deliver in movies, none of the peripherals will follow.

The Number Crunching

In his Eventful career, Shahrukh Khan has earned money, love, awards and enough numbers. Whenever he goes to a press conference or an event, people attach numbers to gauge his popularity and stardom by saying number 1 or number 2. People attach numbers to gauge his business proposition because of the success he had in terms of outside outlook for the material stuff that he had gained whether its glamorous IPL Cricket team, Brand endorsements, Production Company or commercially successful films. Every time his films releases, people talk about 100 crore or 200 crore box- office collection. However, Shahrukh Khan does not believe in numbers at all and finds it disturbing sometimes. He never use numbers as a gauge for human beings or films. He just want to know the bottom line. "My whole struggle with life, if there is any struggle in this wonderful life that I lead, is not to be controlled by numbers," he said.

He has passion for things. He has no understanding about numbers. He has said several times that only telephone have numbers. He does things, which gives him happiness. Even in Business, numbers does not drive him. He has a belief that if you are doing a business in terms of numbers, you are limiting yourself. If the business is meant in terms of numbers, then sky is not the limit.

Cinema is a creative field. He believes that numbers is now confining everything. People, who talk about numbers, keep on trying to confine the free flights of creativity and beauty that he wants to create through work. People, who do not understand creativity, reduce the importance of it by giving them numbers. They sometimes set up a parameter or measure to an art form or creation by putting numbers. According to him, Numbers are given to understand creativity at a basic level. These are outside point of view. There is some sort of creativity that everyone possess and if it gets bog down by numbers then it is over.

He does not like to equate success with tangibility. He truly believes that if your creativity is going to be tangible in terms of money, then you are limiting yourself. You put a limit to what you can do in life. A creative person cannot be slave to numbers. He strongly believes that if you become slave to numbers, you are just running after something, which is extremely tangible and utterly boring. "Numbers should be like your favorite pet dog who keeps following you. You can't follow them," he mentioned.

In Modern era, everything is equated with money. When a film releases, it's incredible opening gets everyone's attention. There was a time when Hindi films used to have silver jubilee or golden jubilee. Those days have gone now. It is very common to say that film has made 100 crore or 200 crore benchmark though a very few people know the real business of cinema from outside. It has become a benchmark for the Indian films. It has become game of numbers. No one talks about film. Shahrukh Khan believes that this benchmark is not something that you compete; it is something that encourages everyone to believe that you can conquer new territories of business, which is good for the Indian film Industry.

Being a romantic hero, he does not deal in numbers or figures. He does not equate the result of a film in terms of numbers. He does not bother about the commercial aspect of the film. He does not like to reduce cinema to just few basic numbers. He is a person who deals with feelings. When he does a film, he leaves a part of him in it. It is an extension of himself and when this extension is measured in stupid numbers whether it falls in lakhs or crores, it does not somehow make him feel very important about his own feelings. He does films, which he likes to do and want people to see them. When many people see them, lots of numbers come but the bottom-line is it was nice, it was entertaining, and that is why people saw them.

His endeavor is to tell a story, which touches heart and make everyone laugh. He has always felt that the audience should enjoy his films. He feels sad when they do not enjoy. He does his job and leave the rest on the audience because he believes that the best judge of any kind of art form or creativity is the perceiver. He just hopes it reaches out to everyone in the audience. He thinks that if a film is measured by the amount of money it makes, then people have no right to ask, "Where is good cinema." The story, acting, songs, enactments are not measurable. When the money is made, there will be comparisons made by people who like to think film just as a commodity. Each individual film is liked for its own uniqueness and has its own time, space and place. Each film is same if we start equating them with some measure of money. However, Businessmen have to do it but it should not become the talking point of a film.

100 Crore Club: A Mere Nomenclature

Actor turned producer Shahrukh Khan Calls 100 crore club a compartmentalize nomenclature. A category or cubicle has been created, which is useless. He believes that we like to compartmentalize things. Everybody likes to have an identity. It makes us feel very easy. It helps us to deal with life. A part of it is now crept into films, which the actor thinks is completely wrong. It has been put forward. They are not the creative aspect. It takes away any aspect of creativity from cinema. He believes that People who do not understand art or creativity in films, they put their work in these clubs or category. They are reducing the level of creative people as well as level of hope for business by calling a film 100 crore.

Being Creative and serious actor at times, Shahrukh Khan believes that it is a narrow way of thinking in terms of business. To think of it is a limitation by itself. If you need to dream, then you should dream like the industrialists. The true people, who are into the business of cinema, should dream ₹10,000 crore. "If I have to give myself a number, I like to call it ₹10,000 crore in a week," he said. That is an honest dream. They should think of increasing the number of cinema. They should think of density per cinema of number of people. That is how the business will increase. He has always maintained that numbers are always going to change as big movies keep coming because screens and platforms are increasing. Therefore, these 100 crore or 500 crore will keep changing. The longevity of the film is dependent on how nice the film is. What makes him happy is the fact that people enjoys the film, which is more heartening than the numbers.

Selling Dreams

People call Shahrukh Khan a fierce businessman. He has been put on the list of most powerful people of the world. In May 2014, a research company Wealth X tagged him as the second richest actor in the world. Many people address him as one of the Top most young entrepreneur of India but the actor does not consider himself as an entrepreneur. He claims that he does not understand business. He has never thought of things like this. He thinks that it is a misnomer for people who think he is a good businessperson. He just feels a lot of ownership in what he does. He has no idea how to handle finance. He is too easy on negotiations and contracts. He can give a number of Ideas. His mind is a fertile ground for new ideas and thoughts, which are about youthful people. He can think of different ideas in seconds and knows very well how to deliver them into reality. He believes that an idea is bigger than anything else in the world. Sometime he goes to office and ask the team can we do this, can we do that?

Business is related to passion that he has for his products. The passion drives him to run a business. "I only enter into a business or an association where I think I have some kind of passion for it. It may not be the ultimate passion like I have for acting but I never get into a business, which is fly-by-night. I don't get into a business where somebody tells me *2 lagaega 500 kamaega* (invest two will earn five hundred)," he mentioned.

Shahrukh Khan is passionate about entertainment, children and sports. These things turned him on. He enjoys creating things for these three parts. Whenever he gets an opportunity to invest in any of these things, he always do without thinking about the business aspect of it. His businesses are the passion he has. He understands entertainment and loves children. With Kidzania, he got the opportunity to mix entertainment with children. He is sportsman by nature. He always wanted to be a sportsman. He still plays games and tries to be fit. With Kolkata knight riders, he brings entertainment with sports. Film production, of course, is an extension that he owes it to himself.

In a small way, Shahrukh Khan tries to sell dreams, which are a little more intangible. He tries to keep it real and simple. If he finds a good product, he takes it to the Consumer with aggressive entertainment. He believes that if you have a product that you believe in, you should live with it. If there is a movie or any part of a creative work, you need to own it, stand by it and die with it. You do not disown it. If you can do that, then business will follow.

Shahrukh Khan believes that the best of the business plans may not work because Cinema or art is always going to measure on the anvil of how people react to it subjectively. The actor meets successful business people of various fields. Apart from hobnobbing with them, he studies and visits their business places. Whenever he goes and meet these successful people, he gets intrigued by the way they run their businesses. He gets so amazed that there is no limit of their businesses. He still have not been able to successfully apply the business strategies from these businesses to his creative businesses because filmmaking is a different business. It cannot be completely corporate. It needs to have a little personal touch.

It is like running a big house where one need professional help of cleaners, sweepers and other people who set it up but it should still feel like a family house. Somehow, what he learnt from businesses is that you need certain amount of professionalism in filmmaking but it needs to have a personal touch.

9

Rise of Indian Cinema

In India, Politics, Cricket and films are the three ruling entertaining things but the lion's share of entertainment belongs to the films. Cinema, in India, is not just a form of entertainment;it is really a religion. It is a way of life. There is such an exciting experience when a new movie of a big star comes. People go crazy. Films are not just part of entertainment; it is an integral part of their life. Nobody, in India, can ignore cinema. It is deeply rooted in Indian culture.

India has a very strong film industry. People are clearly associated with it. It has its own language and way of seeing things. The Hindi film industry has made films on every subject in keeping with the changing times, whether they were social themes, political or filled with emotions. The films, someway, talks about the goodness of life and it has good making and traditional values. Indian movies contain exotic elements like melodramatic themes, lavish sets, colored costumes, exaggerated violence, dialogues, romance, songs, dance routines and many others. These movies have close insights into Indian society. The younger generation follows them. They are spicy and irresistible mixture to which the Indian moviegoers are addicted. They are full of universal emotions like love, goodness and family. They talk about hope and happiness. They are about celebration of life. Nobody can question the credibility, goodness and greatness of the Indian film industry. It has the potential to entertain the world audience. It has the capability to spread the message of Love and happiness within a form of entertainment.

The Indian Film Industry: Largest and Earliest

The Indian film industry is known as the largest film industry in the world, in terms of number of films released annually. Maximum numbers of films are made in different languages, which include Hindi, Punjabi, Marathi, Bengali, Tamil, Telugu, Kannada, Malayalam, Assamese and others. Millions of tickets are sold every day with bigger share going to Bollywood- India's dream factory.

Hindi cinema (or Bollywood) shows the experience of the whole Indian Cinema. There has been a global acceptance of Hindi movies. There is a huge Indian audience in countries like US, UK, Canada, Indonesia, Malaysia, Morocco, the Middle East and some other territories. In countries like Sweden, Poland, Austria and Germany, many non-Indians watch Hindi movies. These all represent a big market for Bollywood movies.

The Indian film industry is one of the earliest film industries in the world. In 2013, cinema of India has completed its 100 glorious years. Its birth is attributed to the Lumiere Brothers, who are known as the inventors of cinema. In 1896, the Lumiere films had shown in Bombay (Now Mumbai). These short films inspired many directors. However, the credit for making the first indigenous Indian feature film was attributed to Dadasaheb Phalke-the father of Indian cinema. He made the first full-length Indian silent film 'Raja Harishchandra', based on the legend Raja Harishchandra that was released on 3rd may 1913. Since then the Indian film industry has come a long way.

Earlier, people were not open to watch movies. They had never acknowledged the existence of cinema. Amitabh Bachchan, the Indian superstar of his generation, has mentioned in several forums that there was a time when acting in Hindi films was not considered a noble profession in India. The profession of an Engineer or a doctor was considered as a noble one but not many people wanted to become film actors. Those who wanted to work in movies used to feel very scared and hesitant. That time has changed now. There has been a change in the mindset of the people. The Indian audiences are now aware of the importance of cinema in their lives.

Cinema, in India, has reached at a level where it is commercially viable. It is a great business proposition and it is getting more professional now. It has established itself in the form of Industry. It is a remarkable change. A very decent and educated people are coming to make a career in the Indian film industry. It has come to a stage to respect like any other profession. People from the entertainment field get lot of love and respect from the audience. A huge amount of recognition is given to them. It is a great profession if people like it.

Bollywood and Hollywood movies are far different from each other but they do share many similarities. Like Western movies, the name of the game for Bollywood movies is Escapism. India is a developing nation or on the threshold of huge development. The escapist plots of Bollywood movies are not yet fantastic. It is not completely imaginative. It is still not real imagination. They are still in touch with reality. The aspirations are very small. The dreams are attainable. The fantasies or escapism that they offer are too limited and a little more real like having a regular job, buying a car, making a big house and settling down with wife and having children. Very simple and basic things, which developed nation takes for granted, an ordinary Indian person likes to acquire. The greatest achievement that an ordinary person in India can have is hope for Ferrari, not hope for flying to the moon.

On the other hand, Hollywood films are larger than life. Their ecstasies, fantasies and hopes are bigger because they have already achieved so much fantastic things in real life. Fantasy and escapism has always been the key of contemporary Hollywood cinema, with series like "Batman," "Superman" and "Spiderman."

Shahrukh Khan is very thankful to the Indian film Industry as his whole existence in the world is because of Indian Cinema. Everything that he stands for is because of Indian cinema. He wants to work in a way for the future of Indian film Industry. He needs to do it just for the fact that he has been working in Indian cinema for so many years. He wants to do new things in any part of filmmaking by doing which he feels satisfied at the end of his career. He has good feelings of making movies and love people who make movies.

Art and Commercial Sensibilities

In any point in the history of Indian Cinema, one will find two kind of sensibilities- Art and Commercial.

Normally, Art Cinema is known for its serious content. It presents a realistic way of life. It includes a relatively small proportion of people. However, it does not earn a lot of money but it requires smart people and thinking. It does not attract people too hard. It is not very loud but people enjoys it and discuss about it because it is very difficult to express heart-felt things. It is very difficult to analyze non-existing intangible things and put them into some kind of words and emotions.

India is a diverse country where people are not extremely rich in some places and the Indian audience varies from the very young to the very old to the educated to the very uneducated. When people go to watch a film, they like to think it as an event for the whole family. They want to watch a film, which include the interest of their own. Thus, there need to have a little bit of action, comedy, songs, dance, crying, happiness and a big climax. It is like a cabaret variety show, which is the commercial part of cinema and where everything is put together in one film. All the genres of Hindi film can be seen in one commercial film. In addition, it requires actors to be trained in the art of acting, dancing and having fun. It gives everything in one package.

Commercial cinema is the most dominant feature of Indian Cinema. In India, commercial films are more viable and expensive to make. The actors talk loudly about their movies in order to get huge number of people to come and watch it. In addition, lot of thinking requires to make a commercial film, which makes money.

Earlier, Art Cinema was known as parallel Cinema because they were running side by side of mainstream commercial cinema. Therefore, there has never been a collaboration. Though Art Cinema is getting space in Indian cinema but it is still very less as compared to the commercial cinema.

Bollywood star Shahrukh Khan trained in an English theatre. Being a theatre actor, He understands both- the meaningful cinema as well as the commercial cinema but he enjoys the louder commercial cinema. The kind of cinema that he has done is heavily commercial and totally for entertainment. He is more inclined towards it. He plays different characters in the parameter of Commercial Cinema. He tries to make films within some parameters of what everybody can watch. In addition, he has made some issue based films with songs, dances and with the trappings and parameters of hugely popular commercial cinema.

RA.ONE

Bollywood movies are lagging behind the Hollywood movies in number of things like technology, screenplay and movie marketing. There is a huge gap between them. The visionary Shahrukh Khan, on countless occasion, spoken about the need to develop new style of filmmaking. He is one of the few Indian actors who have tried to reduce the gap between Bollywood and Hollywood. He had taken risk and initiative to develop a new style of filmmaking. He is involved with his big name colleagues to push the Indian film Industry forward. He wants to bring class and international scale to his movies. He wants to make films that appeal to both Indian and international audiences. He believes that he can be one of those leading filmmakers from India who can make purely Indian film and get the whole world to watch it.

In 2011, He made science fiction superhero movie *Ra.one* that was the most technologically complex Hindi movie. It was the most expensive Indian film at the time of release. The movie was directed by director Anubhav Sinha and Co-Produced by Eros Entertainment and Red Chillies Entertainment. He made it at a very big level. It was made with high standards of special effects and state of the art technology. Visual Effects were extensively used in the movie. It played an important part in the whole making process of the movie. Red Chillies'sVFX Division was responsible for it. There were the people who were very good in the VFX aspect of filmmaking. They sorted out most of the problems. Whenever the movie filmmakers felt short or disappointed, they came out with solutions. The style and execution of Ra.one's visual effects were refined and dynamic. Major part of the film's production budget was utilized on it. Due to this, finally the film looked beautiful.

Shahrukh Khan took a huge risk to make this movie. He is a big believer of the fact that higher you go, higher the risk you should take. He likes to take chances. As being one of the biggest name of the Indian cinema, Shahrukh Khan has always said that "If we don't take the chances, who else will."

He is among those actors who are in the position of choice. "If you are in the position of choice and if you don't make the choices which can change things that you work in, I think that will be the most limiting factor of an actor," he said. The actor believes that nobody remembers you for the small successes. If you go wrong, let people remember you for the mistake that you make. They might remember you for the big mistake or while making those big mistakes, you might make the biggest success possible. "You got to believe in life that if you are to end, you got to end making a big failure rather than a small success"

In his filmy career, Shahrukh Khan played everything- from action hero to romantic lover to ruthless villain but he confessed several times that he always wanted to be either Spiderman or Batman while growing up. "I come from a lower middle class background, always wanted to be a superhero. I didn't know what excuse to use to make a film of this genre, which is not very popular in India- science fiction cum superhero. I didn't have the budgets. I didn't have the status or even the resources. Then, my children grew up so, I found the excuse first. Now, I can say my kids would want a film like this but actually the truth is I wanted to make one," he said.

In India, the superhero genre is completely new and perhaps not the popular one. One of the basic idea was to bring superhero in India. It was devised to bring a new genre in India and to please a very young set of children. There were several cool quotients for the youngsters. That is, for Shahrukh Khan, the biggest high to create something, which Indian cinema wants to see in terms of technology.

Ra.one's story follows Shekhar Subramaniam (Shahrukh Khan), an expert video game designer, who is unable to bond with his son Prateek. His son considers him nothing but a sense of embarrassment. To please his son, Shekhar invent a Motion-sensor based game in which the villain (Ra.one) is more powerful than the protagonist (G.one). In addition, it manages to bridge the distance between the father-son duos. However, just as that happens, the villain (Ra.one) from the game comes to the real world. Here, Ra.one's mission is to eliminate his first opponent gamer Lucifer that is his son in real life too. How the kid is chased throughout and how the superhero of the game (G.one) is made to appear in reality and fight against Ra.one forms the rest of the Story.

It was an effort, which Shahrukh Khan and his team had taken to create something indigenously, which is interesting for people to watch. It was a step in the direction to make films look better. They had the capability and opportunity to push the bar a little and became pioneer of creating some new kind of cinema in India. There were highly complex sequences in the movie involving a train sequence in which the protagonist G.one runs on the outside of train, passes people on the door and jumps from one train to another. There were also cool sequences, extra-ordinary special effects, stunning car chase and action scenes.

Shahrukh Khan sincerely believes that the main thing in filmmaking is belief. He says this to everyone that sometimes you have to move you knowledge aside to make some space for your belief. Thus, he shifted his knowledge and mathematics to make room for his belief for ra.one. He earned a special place in the history of Hindi Cinema by making this movie. He not only lifted the standard of Hindi cinema but also gave new definition to it. It was the most ambitious venture of his filmy career. He pushed boundaries with that film. It would not be an overstatement to say that he has put Hindi cinema on the map by making this movie. Internationally, he made people from the sub-continent very proud that India can produce, direct and write films like that.

The film was an attempt to set new standards for visual effects in India. Its VFX was locally done in India. For Shahrukh Khan, *Ra.one*, which was also released in 3D, showed how India can now compete with the best in the world. The visual effects of the movie had appreciated by everyone. "Visual Effects will become an integral part of filmmaking. It will be safer for actors. Production costs will be lower. We shot Chakde's finale with 20 persons in the stadium but managed the effect of a lakh. Imagine the cost if we really had to bring one lakh people," he said in an interview with journalist Bharti Dubey.

With this experiment, he kept in touch with the fundamentals of Modern cinema. The movie defined the cinematic language for the coming period in India. He entered into an entirely new area of filmmaking. Technically, the movie was an absolute wonderment. It was a step in the direction to make films look better. It reflected a beginning of a new trend in popular Indian Cinema. The movie changed how people see and perceive visual effects in India. It was a sign of new Digital age. It was devised to bring the superhero genre into the country. The movie received number of awards for its technical aspects including the 59th National film award for best special effects.

Shahrukh Khan used to get agitated with the fact that the Indians, in abroad, are a little embarrassed of Indian films. "Whenever I travel, I see some other films and having done 70 films, I am like my film does not look like this, our film do not look like this. So it is important for me to do that (Ra.one) for that reason," he mentioned once.

In 2008, the hugely popular Oscar winning *Slumdog Millionaire*, which was shot in India, presented the images of India. It was a British made film, which was not uniformly liked in India. Its depiction was questioned because some believed that this film was selling the poverty of India. The film, that had charmed audiences around the world, depicted slum dwellers in a bad light. Some people said that the movie was showing the wrong side of India. This was not the India that should shown abroad. This was not a movie that people would like to see as Hindi cinema. Many Indians around the world criticized it.

At once, Shahrukh Khan wanted to make *Slumdog Millionaire* under his own production house in India for Indian people. It was offered to him because he was hosting the Indian version of 'Who wants to be a millionaire?' at that time. Later, things did not work out and he turned down the opportunity but He liked the story. He liked the simplicity and smartness of the film that there are 10 questions and somehow those 10 things happened to you in life. In his opinion when a Western unit comes to India, they do not want to sell the sadness of India. They just amazed by the difference in lifestyle of Indians and the West. In addition, he thinks that we cannot deny and get disturbed if somebody come and shot in slums of India.

At the same time, the actor believes that an Indian filmmaker selling the sadness of India is unfair because he does not want to sell the sadness of India. He wants to present different colors of India to the world. He wants to tell and highlight the other aspects of India because he knows India well enough. He wants to tell the story of India, which is educated and colorfully cultured."I don't want to sell the poverty, the culture and the snake charmers of India. I want to sell the educated middle class of India. I want to tell them there is a lot of intelligence here, intellect here, rich here, happiness here, colorful culture here," he said.

Retaining Indian film viewership

Principle movies, all around the world, are Hollywood movies. They are essentially made for the global audience. India is the country where local cinema does better than the international cinema. It is the only market where Hollywood movies struggle to compete. Shahrukh Khan always has a worry that if the Indian Cinema is not changed quickly enough, it would be overtaken by Hollywood cinema.

Hollywood, the cinema of United States, has a profound effect on cinemas across the world. Wherever you go, people wants to see Hollywood productions. Many Hollywood movies are making majority of their revenue outside the United States. They have taken over everywhere. The quality of Hollywood movies are of world class standards and they are designed in a way so that it appeals to the global audience. They spends more money on great effects and graphic processes of the movie. They make high budget films on a consistent basis. Many believes that good screenplay writing and better use of technology are the reasons of their success.

As a result of Globalization, India is offering enough space for the Hollywood entertainment to come and display their movies. Indian viewers are able to experience Hollywood movies with the help of fast spread wireless communication and new media technologies.

The Indian audience are becoming increasingly familiar with the Hollywood entertainment. The youth of India is growing up on watching Hollywood Superheroes. A big part of their business comes from India. They have been highly successful in penetrating the Indian market in various possible ways.

There is no question that the Hindi film industry is in trouble. Over the years, India has seen significant increase in the young and urban population that had exposure to Hollywood entertainment. Wherever Hollywood has gone, they have destroyed their film industry. In countries like Britain, France, Italy or Germany, the local cinema has been taken over by the more popular commercially wonderful Hollywood cinema. The culture of Europe match a lot to the culture of America. Thus, their stories are acceptable here. India is one of the few countries where the local cinema survives in spite of Hollywood. Bollywood actor Shahrukh Khan wants to retain this Indian film viewership intact because that is one of the only entertainment things in India. His concern is to hold on the Indian audience for Hindi cinema. "I think there is a danger. We will lose Indian audiences for Indian films very soon. The western inflow, westernization of culture is already happening. There are genres of films which if we don't venture into, our young audience will start looking for them in foreign films. Gradually, as in Italy, China, Japan and Korea, people here won't watch local films, unless we spruce up our technology. That's my main objective as a producer," he opined.

Shahrukh Khan wants to maintain India's cinematic individuality. He wants to retain the cinema culture of India. "We shouldn't dumb down our cinema. We should maintain our culture. Song and dance is part of our culture. That's the USP of our films. That's the reason we have movie stars in this country. You don't have the star system anywhere in the world apart from Hollywood. We have it because of the culture of our cinema," he said in an interview to film fare on completing 100 years of Hindi Cinema in 2013.

There are many genres, which the Indian cinema have not been able to tap. Actor Producer Shahrukh Khan wants to bring new genre to the Indian cinema so that the youth of India stick to it. He believes that there is a need to introduce genres like science fiction, action and horror so that Indian youngsters do not look down upon the Indian movies and feel proud that Bollywood entertainment is being able to match the Hollywood entertainment. There is a need to bring different kind of entertainment for different people in the country. Ra.one was a step in that direction. The effort for this film was to retain the Indian audience first. The film was made as per international standards and was very good looking on that front. The actor thinks that the inputs of technology, new ways of storytelling and making it more exciting for the youth can help Indians to stick to its Cinema. The kind of technology that Indian filmmakers use is not as per International standards and the people are accepting it. The actor believes that it is the high time to stop saying, "it is good enough for Hindi films." If we do not stop saying that, we will lose Hindi film audience because they are watching International films much more in numbers than before.

Knowledge Sharing

The basic idea to make Ra.one was to bring Superhero in India. It is genuinely a step forward in terms of how Indian movies are made in terms of technology, camera or sound. There was a huge difference in the quality and that happened because it was a collaborative process with International technicians and Indians. The soul of the movie was the fact that a group of people like actors, director, writers, action-directors, VFX supervisors, technicians, sound-designers and many others have worked together and believed that they are doing a different kind of film. The actor believes that still they have long way to go to create superhero franchise in India and one of the aspect of making this movie was that post this movie, there should be a set of at least 200 people who know how to make a film like this.

In that way, Shahrukh Khan encouraged knowledge sharing of latest filmmaking techniques of this genre to create more excellent VFX work in films and to strengthen VFX studios in India. Later, Red Chillies VFX division created VFX for *Krrish3* (2013). Shahrukh Khan was feeling honored that he was involved in some part of the work of *Krissh3* as a VFX studio.

Globalization of Indian Cinema

Shahrukh Khan is extremely proud of Indian Cinema. He sees the world as a market for Indian cinema. He thinks that India has the capability, talent, desire, infrastructure and drive to take the Indian Cinema all around the world. He truly believes that Indian filmmakers has nice stories to tell and has amazing amount of culture to show. The Indian movie Industry can become the global powerhouse of entertainment. He strongly feels that it is the Indian film Industry, which will dominate global entertainment. India can be a global entertainment portal. Cinema of India is so thriving and vibrant. It can be used as a global asset for India. He wants Indian Cinema to reach every corner of the world while retaining the culture, warmth and colors that it has.

Shahrukh Khan believes that the globalization of Indian cinema means the globalization of India or Indian culture. Cinema is the face of a country. Normally, when a country is progressing, the first thing that comes to fore is its culture. India, with all its richness, beauty and humanity, is depicted in Hindi films. Its diverse culture is depicted in Hindi films. Bollywood stands for the packaging of India. It is the packaging of a country and even arguably the most interesting thing for an outsider. If somebody visits a country, he or she wants to know their people's language, what they wear and how do they sing and dance rather than the economy and Sensex figure of that country. In a way, the first thing they get to know or wants to know is their culture.

Shahrukh Khan does not believe in crossover films. He believes that there is nothing like a film that can go from here to there. A film should take the whole world and make for an international audience. "In all this wonderful happenings around the world of entertainment there is this one word, which I keep hearing from Indian filmmakers to which I have an aversion and I would like to try and remove it from the vocabulary of Indian films. I would just like to make a mention of that and then move onto more positive thinks about international cinema and us that one word or term that disturbs me is that all Indian filmmakers keep chasing an elusive dream called the cross over film. There is an action film...a Romantic...a comedic or a dramatic film...a bad film...a completely vulgar and cheap film but I have never understood what is a crossover film? I think it is nothing at all. There is nothing known as a crossover film Because if there was, Hollywood our smarter cousin would have already started making crossover films made in America and taken over the Indian film market," he said by adding that "Instead of going forward with our desire to cross over we should think of taking over. Actually, we should be thinking of globalizing Bollywood films because Globalize we must and to do that we need a give and take relationship with western cinema, especially Hollywood. It is essential."

Cinema is a story telling technique. As far as entertainment is concerned, the rest of the world has moved ahead in terms of storytelling techniques. The Indian cinema still stick to what they have been doing for years in terms of their techniques. They have not taken steps forward. Being a theatre actor, Shahrukh Khan is a big believer of telling a story. According to him, if we keep western cinema in mind, the storytelling techniques need to improve a lot more in India. Bollywood films have fantastic stories but they are less brief in storytelling. The actor believes that the storytelling is good but storytelling techniques needs to improve a lot. It is a science in west and the Indian filmmakers have not conquered it yet. Therefore, the whole idea is to retain the uniqueness but the whole formatting of storytelling should be a little more international.

The actor believes that there is a need to format Indian films in a way that suits watching it internationally. He believes that the Hindi film industry makes film in all kinds of unique systems, which is good but it is not the format which the International audience or community is looking for. He equated this to being invited to a very upper class British party. He believes that you have to dress up in the way they do. Not everybody is Mahatma Gandhi. You have to show some respect by dressing up in the way they want you to dress up and follow the rules. It is not a big thing. In the same way, if Indian filmmakers wants to go internationally, they have to dress up their films like them. He feels that there is a need to follow the dress code that is existing in the world because that is the larger market at this point of time. We will never achieve an International standard of filmmaking unless we respect the dress code that western audience is used to. "If you want to be on Global cinema, you have to tell the stories you wish to, the songs, the dance that you want to, the expressions that you want to express but you really need to put it in the garb of what the world is used to," he said in a panel discussion with NDTV.

"I think it is highly improbable and highly I think selfish of creative people in this country if we are not able to change ourselves according to the needs and the way they are used to watch cinema or any other kind of art form," he added.

According to Shahrukh Khan, a few things needs to be done to make Bollywood productions as popular as Hollywood films in the global market. To globalize Indian movies, there is a need to make Indian films a less lengthy. The beginning would be to make sure that the films are shorter. They need to be in the format of 90 minutes or 2 hours. Indian timings should not be imposed upon the rest of the world. The westerners are not used to that. The length have to shorten.

Indian films are still in the mode of musicals, which is interesting and different from the world cinema. Shahrukh Khan believes that songs and dance sequences have to remain to globalize Indian cinema because that is the USP of Indian films and that is what comes up in front. They are the defining elements of Indian movies and are extremely popular among the Indian masses. Every cinema, which has made an impact on the world, has an USP. A clear USP of Hong Kong, Chinese and East Oriental cinema is Kung-Fu. In the same way, Song and dance sequences are the USP of Indian cinema. The Indian filmmakers need to careful not to lose what makes our cinema so magical. It should be included in the format. It helps to narrate the story but there is a need to make them a little more realistic.

There is a need to work a lot on screenplay. India does not have great scientific screenplay writers that needs to be develop. It can be develop by taking help from the western writers as they have converted this art form into a science. It is a more developed science in western cinema. There is more video literacy in the western audience. They have been exposed more to videos than the Indian audience. Therefore, there is a need to take help from western world, use their technicians and get them to teach Indian technicians in screenplay.

Celebrating 'Stars': A great Positive

Hindi Cinema- colloquially known as 'Bollywood'- is completely Star driven. It has a very strong star system and the reason for local movies to survive is stardom. Movie stars are the driving force of Indian cinema. There is a huge balance of stardom in India whether it is an actor or a director.

People give too much credit to stars especially in India. There is a huge emotional connection of audience with stars. Of course, a film requires a number of things to become a blockbuster but stardom plays a major part. Wherever there is a star system, the film industry thrives. It invokes interest of the audience. It is just a way of how audience is attracted. It helps to sustain the film Industry. If there is no star system, the interest level of making films starts falling down. The whole system of looking up to someone and trying to find a hero has made Indian cinema survived.

India is one of the few nations besides USA, which has a star system in the film Industry and actor Shahrukh Khan does not consider it a bad thing. According to him, Entertainment has reached a level where you cannot disassociate it from stardom of it at all. "If there is no stardom, there is no film Industry," he said. The actor strongly believes that the star system is an extremely important part of globalization of any industry, not just to the film Industry. In any industry, many things are personality driven and they need personalities to drive especially in the media field. If a film is not personality driven, it will never stay for too long. If the film industry is not personality driven, there would not be a film Industry. Wherever the film Industry has failed, it is because it does not have personalities to take it forward. Therefore, it is a good thing that India has a very strong star system.

Shahrukh Khan often gives the example of Hollywood filmmaker Quentin Tarantino, who once said that the film Industry would only exist in a country on a big scale, if it has a star system. England. France and some other great filmmaking nations somehow have not been able to keep up with rest of the world because star system does not exist there and stars does not experience a high level of deification. The way audience takes the Indian film stars is a little different from the way the audience takes the western star there. Being an actor there is still just a job. "We are considered like 'demi-gods' here, and the reason is not because we are better or good, but because there is no other mode of entertainment in India. So you need to be a little more 'demi-goddy', being an Indian film star. You need to be a little more mystical and you need to be a little more enigmatic," he said. In addition, the "demi-gods" status that has given to the Indian film stars makes greater business sense.

Game changers

India is a diverse nation as far as audience is concerned. They are so varied and knowledgeable. They are the greatest judges because different people, cultures, religions and languages surround them. They have the impression of every culture, custom and language. They choose a film to watch by keeping these things in mind. They are certainly more aware and well informed than before. They are ready for different genres of films. They have the courage and even pay money to watch movies made on different subjects. If an Indian audience likes a movie that means everything is fine in that movie. They are the most intelligent audiences and there are filmmakers especially young filmmakers in the Hindi film Industry who are nearly as intelligent as the Indian audience.

Shahrukh Khan believes that a number of new and young directors have changed the phase of Indian Cinema and because of that Indian Cinema is being recognized everywhere. They have the sensibility and understanding of different modes of storytelling. They have learned the technique and technology of screenplay writing from the western Cinema. They have been able to take those ideas and put them in movies. Although they failed many a times but at least started it in Indian Cinema. They have pushed the technique, craft and art of storytelling to a new level.

The young generation of filmmakers are more confident about their identity. They are quite young in thoughts and execution.

They work with new set of rules, ideas and thoughts. They have the astonishing self-belief that what they are doing is appropriate and correct. They are new thinking people and are exposed to the western cinema. They have made movies in which the western culture is seamlessly blend with traditional Indian family values. They have made low budget generation next movies which deals with subjects of our daily lives as well as having lessons about love and family ties. Unlike the traditional Bollywood love stories, their films make connect with day-to-day problems of the people. Their stories are based upon the fundamental experiences of life. Characters and situations are so related to the real ones. They have made movies, which are significantly deviated from the Bollywood masala movies. Their movies are full of creative stuff, which enables the audience to think carefully. They are able to make movies, which are new and refreshing to the Indian audience as well as Indian community living abroad. In a way, they articulate the dreams of the nation.

A chunk of young filmmakers has begun experimenting with the stereotype of female characters in popular Hindi Cinema. They have made offbeat movies by taking female protagonist as a central character. In this way, they have created a separate space for the actresses. They have taken efforts to present strong female characters with extraordinary themes. They have shown a positive portrayal of Indian woman who is educated, confident and lives life on his own terms.

Technology: The next step

Shahrukh Khan is very fortunate enough that he has been a part of Indian cinema at times and era when it has gone through some amazing innovation in terms of style, innovation and storytelling. As a filmmaker, he has a huge interest in trying to bring technology into Hindi cinema. He has a broader outlook in place when it comes to technology. He is quite open to new technologies and devices. Given the huge competition in the International market, he has a huge interest in trying to bring technology as a producer into

Indian Cinema. He finds ways to push technology and to use it more effectively.

Shahrukh Khan believes that the quality part of a film should be of the highest order. Apart from the content, one of the thing that Indian filmmakers can control is the technology. No one can control the business, story or result of the film. Cinema should look comparable to cinema of the world specifically Hollywood. There is a need to control how the film looks, keeping the content Indian and honest.

India is the only country in the world, which still has regional audiences. The actor believes that the only way by which we can retain our Hindi Cinema is by increasing technology. He wants to go to the next level of filmmaking in terms of technology. He wants the Indian film industry to look at technology closely and use it in a better way.

Shahrukh Khan wants to make a symbiotic relationship with Hollywood. He wants to take a lot of technology from Hollywood to India. He thinks that there is a need to accept the fact that Western cinema are ahead of Indian Entertainment technologically. He believes that there is a need to learn about the technology, ideas and tricks from western media and entertainment as they have witnessed technological innovations at least a decade ahead of India. The Indian film industry needs to operate with more mindsets that are international. It is the west, which can show ways to the cinema of India. "If we don't innovate in terms of technology, the science of marketing and writing this market will dwindle. That is why we don't need Hollywood investment as much as we need their knowledge," he said. As a producer, he wants to take technology and screenplay knowhow from west so that he can make a better Indian film.

The actor feels that there is a huge backlog for the Indian film Industry to cover up before jumping into new technologies. Firstly, there is a need to hold up the technology that the Indian film Industry have not mastered yet. There is so much to learn in terms of Camera, lensing, Editing, Lighting, Visual-effects and Special effects to make Indian films truly International.

Collaboration: A Great idea

Shahrukh Khan believes that one aspect which Indian film Industry lack is collaboration between different artists. Collaboration is extremely important to enhance the art, commerce and the whole idea of storytelling. The bottom line is to tell a story, to tell a song or an expression. There has never been a collaboration between a commercial filmmaker and an intellectual person in the Indian film Industry. The Collaborative process is an important step forward. He believes that unless the Indian artists from the film industry develop a habit of collaborating with each other, they will never be able to globalize the Indian cinema.

Indian cinema has great stories to tell. His logic is that the business acumen of the Americans or westerners and storytelling capabilities of this side of the world would be a great mix.

10

Because My Name is Khan

On 15th august 2009, India was celebrating its 63rd Independence Day. On this day, Shahrukh Khan made the headlines for not what he does on screen but for what he does off it. The US Immigration officials detained Shahrukh Khan, a global icon, at the Newark Liberty International Airport, America, when he was heading towards a parade celebrating India's Independence Day. He was flying from Newark, New Jersey to Chicago, when he was pulled out of a security line. He was detained after his name appeared in a computer-generated list and questioned for nearly two hours of what the US called racial profiling to read out terror suspects. He was subjected to intensive questioning about the purpose of his visit to America.

The news came as a shock for millions of Shahrukh Khan fans. The Indian media showed the Shahrukh Khan Detention episode with 'breaking news' all over, along with reactions from Bollywood personalities, Indian politicians and security experts. This was not quite a good news for many Indians living all around the world. It upset everyone in the country very much.

The actor surmised that it was because of his last name, in other words, his Muslim identity. His last name showed up on a computer alert list. He said, "I was taken to a room for questioning. They said my name kept popping up on the computer. They wanted contact number of people who could vouch for me."

"I told them I was a movie star who had recently visited the US to shoot my film [*My name is Khan*] and that I was here to attend an event but nothing seemed to convince the immigration officer," he said. However, the US immigration officials said it was just a routine stop. The actor was assuming that the country is paranoid with a certain section of religion of the world. The bias was towards his Muslim name, which was a little unfortunate. He also mentioned that it happened to him before. This was not the first time.

Khan said what surprised him was the strange questions that authorities asked him instead of following the proper security procedure. They were asking him somebody has to vouch for his entry into America. That question troubled him the most. He felt disturbed and humiliated. All his papers were in order. He gave name of people with whom he had finalized a deal. He was allowed out only after Indian embassy intervened and vouched for him. He felt a little ill at ease as a human being. He had not taken it as a personal affront, but it was a little embarrassing for him. His self-respect was hurt.

The actor respected the fact that rules needed to follow. He truly respects that a country need to secure about their borders. He understands the need for Security as the country had gone through huge security threat. A country has to be careful specifically with the things that have happened but also added, "The attitude, obviously, is better to be safe than sorry but in that, may be, You do tend to elongate the process for regular people who want to be if not welcome at least feel not un-welcomed when they come to your country."

Both US and India were quick to react. The Ministry of External affairs in India had taken up the matter with the US Consulate. In New-Delhi, US ambassador to India, Timothy J. Roemer said, "the US Embassy was trying to ascertain the facts of the case- to understand what took place. Shahrukh Khan, the actor and global icon, is a very welcome guest in the United states."

"Many Americans love his films," he added.

What was significant about Khan's experience not simply that it happened? Indeed, prominent Indian travelers including former Indian president Dr. APJ Abdul Kalam and Indian Nobel laureate

Amartya Sen have been victims of racial profiling at airports and countless other Indian and other south Asian travelers have subjected to similar forms of profiling and scrutiny. These incidents caused much anger among Indians and world over.

In reference to the frisking of President A P J Abdul Kalam earlier, Shahrukh Khan said, "I can handle this but when you have someone as respectable as an ex-president getting frisked, I am nobody."

Internationally, and particularly in India, the frisking incident had generated a lot of attention and anger at the harassment of a man widely considered an International icon. The Indian media and the whole country condemned the way he was treated. The Indian film fraternity came out in support and openly expressed their displeasure to this incident. The Indignity he suffered had led to demonstrations and burnings of US flags in protest while others marched on streets with his posters. The story was front-page news in India.

Information and Broadcasting Minister Ambika Soni suggested same kind of treatment to Americans when they visit India. She said, "In our opinion we are frisked more than is necessary in the United States of America. I have always thought that we should frisk them as much as they do us."

"If you want to give a tit-for-tat policy to American actors, then call me to frisk Angelina Jolie and Megan Fox whenever they are visiting India." The actor commented on Ambika Soni advocating a tit-for-tat policy with the US after what he went through.

Shahrukh Khan was never against of rules. He always abides all rules wherever he goes. This is evident from his own words, which he said in an interview to a well-known Indian-American journalist Fareed Zakaria "if I am planning to come to your house, I have to follow the rules. I am very practical like that. If I have to come to your house and you have a rule that I need to take off my shoes before I walk into your study, then I do that." His only question was if the country is so advanced, they should also keep records of people who come there often.

The actor pointed out that the security of any country is important but caste, religion or race should not come in the way of security measures. He is lucky that he has access to friends in the Indian consulate whom he could call up. However, hundreds of others do not have this facility.

In India, there is no culture of accountability. What we have instead is a VIP culture.

It seems to be a uniquely Indian phenomenon. Here, everyone tries to be a VIP. 'Don't you know who I am' culture demands privileges. Politicians and celebrities often claim certain special privileges. A different set of rules applies to them. When asked by CNN-IBN Editor-in-chief Rajdeep Sardesai "Do you believe in VIP culture?" Shahrukh Khan answered, "I always stand in cues. I make my children stand in cues. I have never called a person and said please get me inside faster to any place including a night club." When asked him "When you were being detained, did you ever say to any of those officers `don't you know who I am`?" he said, "I die before saying something like that."

Ironically, the incident happened at time when he was in the process of making the movie *My Name is Khan* (2010), which interestingly had a similar storyline of racial profiling post 9/11. Some people had gone to the extent of calling the Shahrukh Khan Detention episode a publicity stunt. Shahrukh Khan denied that the detention drama was a publicity stunt for his movie. "I don't think that I need publicity" he responded adding "he does not even consider being detained and questioned as a matter of pride." In addition, He said that the film's issue is much larger than just detention at an Airport.

After this incident, when Shahrukh Khan arrived at the Mumbai airport, a huge crowd of his fans and a big media contingent had also gathered to welcome him. He waved, smiled and gave his trademark salaam to the crowd.

When he was asked in a press conference about his detention happened because of his name or religion, the heartthrob of many people across the world professed his love for religion and country by saying that "I believe in my God and I believe in my country irrespective of what people think of it. I know I am Khan, I am Islamic and I am happy being that. You are Hindu and your name is Ravi. You should be very happy being that. That's the way life should be."

11

Be kind to Mankind

Shahrukh Khan is a Religious man. His perspectives on religion are highly admirable. He is a God thanking person more than God-fearing. Since the beginning of his career, He is a huge star with so much love. Therefore, he became a great believer of God and thanks God for all love that he gets. He really thinks that the strongest thing that he has which has made him genuinely very strong is the undying faith in the goodness of God.

Shahrukh Khan believes that Religion is a very personal thing and there is a need to keep it personal. It is a discipline that tells people the way of life and lead them to a higher plane. It is the language for seeking truth. He believes that if we ask for forgiveness, God will forgive us. We do lots of mistakes and wrongs but we have faith and trust in God that he will finally forgive us.

He is proud to be a Muslim and has abiding faith in God. He likes to believe himself as a 'Modern Muslim.' His wife is Hindu. He never tries to impose his religion to her. He fully believes that each religion is about being easy with each other. Being a little liberal minded and educated, he understands the Islam in the way it should be. He has been taught Qur'an from childhood. He has made efforts to understand it and walk the path that God has taught him. He always loves to learn more about Islam. Many a times, Shahrukh Khan says *Inshaallah* (God willing) while speaking. He signs off all his interviews and meetings with *Khuda Hafiz* (May God be your protector).

The actor, on countless occasions, spoken about the virtues of Islamic text and religion in interviews all over the world. His views regarding Islam are clear and correct. He never make statements regarding Islam just because it sounds good. Whatever he says, he really mean it. He has never spoken about Islam in derogatory wrong manner. He feels proud that the young people can take some kind of teachings from his work and through the things that he says about religion.

Secularism

India is an amazingly secular and democratic country. People from different religion are living in this country for years. It is so diverse and yet so together. All the people stick together with all hardships and problems. It makes India a strong nation. Born to Muslims parents in modest circumstances, Shahrukh Khan is very proud to be an Indian. He lives an amazing democratic and secular way of life. He salutes India's diverse culture and its uniqueness to absorb all differences. In his own words, "Indian Civilization does not distinguish in terms of religion. It celebrates uniqueness, differences and absorbs all faiths in its bloodstream. We are not just examples to ourselves, we are an impossible achievement in the world and that's why I feel I am very proud to be an Indian."

Shahrukh Khan is a true face of Indian secularism. His Super clean image is reinforced by his prominent Secularism. He is the living example of India being a secular country. He is known to have Secular religion views and believes in the oneness of god. He believes that the whole point of believing in God by whatever name we address is to have a higher standard of behavior and life. He has been raised in a "mix of religion" and prefers to call himself a 'Secular Indian.' Addressing to people, the actor said, "In the street where I lived, people like Sharmaji have taught me the Gita. In my neighborhood Ram Lilas, I have played the role of a monkey in the monkey army. I was taught Christianity in my school. I made a film on Buddhism [Asoka] with my friends and my wife is a Punjabi Hindu."

The actor has always stood for secularism. He finds no difference in thinking of God. He believes that the basic tanets of all religion are same. His home is secular with the children celebrating all festivals. They are equally familiar with the Gayatri mantra and the Friday prayer. His idea is to think of every religious occasion as a time for everyone to meet and celebrate together and that should be the modern version of Religion.

Shahrukh Khan has always been committed to promote peaceful relations between communities and respect for all human being regardless of their race and religion. These are completely Indian values. He has a secular way of looking at things. He believes that each religion is important but we need to become secular in the way we deal with each other. We all need to understand that we belong to one country, one creed, one caste and one relationship with this country.

As a Muslim superstar in a predominantly Hindu country, Shahrukh Khan believes in Islam and believes that it has some wonderful things. He teaches his son and daughter Islam but he cannot teach them that other religion is not good, better, or worse than Islam.

'Secular' Indian Film Industry

Shahrukh Khan is one of the leading personalities of Indian film Industry. He is Muslim by birth, Islamic by faith and a big star in a Hindu dominated nation. This shows that how Indian Film and Entertainment Industry accepts art without religion coming in the way. Being a Muslim has never been a criterion for becoming an actor or not being an actor. He believes that the Indian film Industry is the most Secular place to find a job for him. He has never been in disadvantage as far as being Muslim is concerned in the film Industry or in India. He is welcomed with open arms whether it is the audience or the filmmakers. He believes that Art and Artists have a tendency to transcend. They do not consider that who is from what community. While acting, the religion is Entertainment, happiness and just telling a story.

The actor maintains that despite living in a country where Muslims are in the minority, he never experienced Prejudice. "In spite of my religion, I have been accepted all over the world. People seem to say that Islam is a minority and, I think, that's quite an ironic statement to make because I have never been made to feel like that. I have been made to feel very special because of my religion. We all need to really trust and believe in our religion whatever religion we belong. I am Islamic by birth so I believe in *Allah* and their sayings and the strange thing is my wife is Hindu so I read the books that she follows or do the *puja* that she does and realize strangely that the language is different but the message is exactly the same," he said in an interview. Nobody has ever asked him 'What religion are you from?' Nobody has ever questioned it and he finds it old fashioned to talk about it in modern India.

Talking about secularism, Shahrukh Khan once said, "This oneness is the beauty of this country. So I would be completely misplaced in my ideology, thought or in the nightmare also to think that someone like me is not appreciated in this country."

Terror and Islam

Islam, by far, is the most eclectic and diverse religion in the world. Post 9/11, it has acquired a separate identity in the world. Unfortunately, Islam is also a religion, which has maximum number of misconceptions. The top most misconceptions are Terrorism and Jihad.

Unfortunately, due to the actions of some misguided Muslims, People think that Islam permit Terrorism. There is insecurity about Islam in the west. The western world perceives Islam as the religion, which propagates terror. The most common question asked by non-Muslim is If Islam is a peaceful religion then why most of the terrorist are Muslims. Every time there is a Terror attack, the Muslim People are asked upon to prove their Patriotism. People gives unworthy opinions and sometimes use bad associations and tags like Muslim Terrorists or Muslim extremists. Shahrukh Khan does not like putting any tag to something. He believes that attachments or association of bad things on someone is not good.

For instance, we say German Tennis Player or German Soccer Team- this represents a good association and inspires many children because the whole world is aware of German sports. That is a good association. However, as soon as, we start labelling bad associations like German killers or Indian rapists, then things goes wrong. It labels a country, a nation or a group, which is wrong. "See actually I have never really thought of an extremist adding any other tag to them- Jewish extremist or an English extremist or an American extremist or a Hindu extremist or a Muslim extremist. Extremist is an extremist. As soon as we start putting, a tag to it is when we are actually inviting trouble. We are inviting trouble in the hearts and in the minds of the people," he said in an interview.

Shahrukh Khan often asked his opinion on terrorism. Maybe because he is a Muslim, people ask him to make sure his opinion is the same as theirs. However, the actor finds this a very strange question because he believes that No one can have two viewpoints about terrorism.

Shahrukh Khan calls Terrorism- a religion of devils and monsters. His father taught him many things like religions do not teach you to quarrel with each other. *Ishwar* and *Allah*, both are God's names. The actor feels that lessons that we learnt from childhood do not mean anything in today's times. Our Religion have tried so hard to show us the right way to live. In spite of that, all these religions have devils and monsters who have made their own religion and he feels that religion is called 'Terrorism.'

"While all civilized religions celebrate and respect life, this new barbaric terror religion loves only death and unfortunately all human faiths now face a challenge," he said at the event organized by the ministry of Home affairs at India Gate in the memory of the victims and heroes of November 26, 2008 Mumbai terror attacks.

Most of the time when any terrorist activity happens, they turn out to be from the Islamic religion. It is a truth that they have to face. The actor, however, accepts the fact that most of the terror attacks in the world are carried out by Muslims. "That's a truth that you have to face. The only way to face it is Yes! they are Muslims but they don't understand Islam properly," he observed. It is the fact that some Muslims are misled by anti-social elements.

Several young people from various countries follow Islam in the name of Jihad. Shahrukh Khan likes to believe that some of them are born Muslim but they are completely misled. They are Muslims by birth but he does not think that they are Muslims by teachings. A big majority of people do not stand for Islam. They stand for their own agenda, political ideology or the issues they have with person-to-person or nation-to-nation.

Shahrukh Khan understands Islamic religion in the way it should be understood. He reads Qur'an in the language that he knows. His parents teaching and his understanding with Islam has made him feel that Islam is an extremely peaceful religion. Thus, He finds it completely shocking that which part of Islamic holy book people have read and figured this out. There is no passage in the holy book, which claims that it is all right to take lives of so many innocent people. There is no religion in this world, which sanction the death of innocent people. There is no God, which gives heaven by doing this. There is no forgiveness in any God of any religion for any terrorist attack.

The teachings of Islam are as wonderful as the teachings of any other religion. The youngsters understand that in a much better way. That is why he has a huge hope in them. He believes that if you can get the youth to behave radically as the terrorists do, you can make sure that the youth of this country can also behave radically in a positive way. He likes to believe that the young Indians are the people who will be truly radical in a constructive sense. When the actor says radical, he does not mean aggressive or killing people. The religion has to be hard work and spreading happiness. There is a need to use the power and anger of youth constructively to have a better country.

When asked, "Is Islam today misunderstood?" in an interview he replied, "Yes, I think it is misrepresented and misunderstood by many. I truly believe that I know a lot of Islam in a modern sense and I teach that to my children but the best part about it is the openness and the secularity that is attached to it. It is misunderstood and sometimes, I think, misused to make an easy statement that, you know obviously, the terrorists must be Islamic. I think that's wrong."

As one of the country's prominent Muslims, Shahrukh Khan believes that Islam does not tell to spread terrorism and to create fear in the minds and heart of the people. He states that people needs to understand that Islam taught about happiness and smiles. It does not in any which way tell you to be violent. It brought about a spiritual awakening through the words of the Prophet. In an interview with Rajdeep Sardesai on CNN-IBN, Shahrukh Khan said that he has read the holy Qur'an. It states that if you heal one man, you heal the whole mankind, and if you hurt one man, you hurt the whole mankind. Nowhere in the Qur'an does it say that Jihad will lead you to Jannat (Paradise). He also added that the book says that in a war, you cannot kill any woman, child, and animal. In addition, you cannot destroy crops. Jihad has supposed to be propagated by the Prophet himself but unfortunately, two versions of Islam exists. There is an Islam from *Allah* and- unfortunately, there is an Islam from the Mullahs. He appeals to all of them to give youngsters, the right reading of the Qur'an.

People, In India, give more acceptable picture of Islam as a religion. It is a widely acknowledged fact that America has terrorist suspects from all nationalities but not from India. There are few radical Muslims in India. They have not succumbed as much. There is something about Indian constitution or system, which gives them a feeling to live peacefully. They are born under a Constitution that protects them and considers as an asset by the politicians when it comes to election. Actor Shahrukh Khan believes that most of the Indian Muslims are Liberal-thinking People. By nature, they are very secular. They are more compromising and understanding. They do give a chance to everyone to say their point of view, listen to it, and not react radically. Of course, there are section of people who do it but that permeates to the Hindus, Muslims, Christians and every section of the society. They do believe that they have the same opportunity to prosper as like people of other religion. Terrorists claims that through terrorism, in some form, they will actually reach heaven but Shahrukh Khan believes that nowhere in Qur'an, which he considers the word of *Allah,* does it say that you are going to be given heaven if you kill harmless and innocent people.

What is Jihad?

One of the greatest misconception in Islam is Jihad. This misconception is not only among the non-Muslims but it is even among the Muslims. Jihad is a common Arabic word which means to strive, struggle and exert effort. In Islamic Context, it means to strive against once own evil inclination. It means to strive to make the society better. It also means to strive in the battlefield for self-defense. According to actor Shahrukh Khan, Fighting and conquering negativity in your heart is the Real Jihad. It is not about killing people on streets.

The Religious Identity

Shahrukh Khan follows the basic tanets of Islam. He takes the core values of the religion. He emphasizes more on feeling Islam than following it. "I just want to know very clearly and I am a Muslim- is it more important for me to look Muslim and see Muslim, or to feel Muslim. I fully respect the scriptures, I fully respect all the *Hadeeths*, I have read the Qur'an in my own way, in Arabic and in English, but I think the time has come, and this genuinely is an appeal, it is more important to feel Muslim, than to look at it. And if you do, it's absolutely cool, and if you don't it's absolutely cool," he said.

"*Namaaz*- I was always taught *niyat se padhi jaati hai* (performed with intention). You have to believe in it yourself. Nobody can teach you. We are taught 5 *waqt ki namaaz padhna zaroori hai* (It is necessary to perform *Namaaz* five times a day), but not every Muslim follows it," he said.

When he was asked, "Do you follow it?"

He replied, "No, I am not able to follow it, and I am very honest about it. I would love to but I can't. I think of Allah every moment of my life."

Politicizing Religion

Shahrukh Khan studied in a catholic school. He has all the practical knowledge about Hindu festivals because he was brought up in a Hindu atmosphere. He used to participate in Ramleela, which is a story of Rama. His wife is a Hindu and his children have been taught the fact that they belong to parents of different religion. Somewhere down the line, it affected his mind. The main thing that he has taken from all these teachings is that we need to be tolerant and patient with each other. We need to respect and love whatever beliefs we have. Khan thinks the normal people understand all this. It is only the people with agendas, politicians, who tries to misuse the power of religion for very small benefits. They are not generally reputed to take religion seriously. They provoke people to talk wrongly in terms of religion to get political mileage. It bothers him deeply that politicians use religion as agenda for explaining their right to rule.

Shahrukh Khan is not a political person at all. He has always said that politicizing religion is the lowest and cheapest trick in the world. The country has been misused at times by the communal disharmony and he feels sad for people who are affected or disturbed because of reason like this. He believes that the power of religion has to use for goodness, kindness and patience. The agendas of leadership need to change to more development, Education and Women Empowerment. These issues should become major political issues, which need to be looked at. "Religion is a very personal thing. It is about faith. It's about you and your God and I don't think anyone in this world has the right to come between you and your God especially politicians," he said at India Today Conclave 2011.

Right Readings of Islam

Shahrukh Khan's parents gave him right readings of Islam. They have explained Islam to him in an extremely nice way. He wants to give right readings of religion to his children because he does not want to take a chance that somebody on the basis of religion misleads his children ever. He does not want to misled them by somebody telling them any different. "I was told like it's nice to go and read the *namaz*. So I would go and do it and, you know, the way it was told was that you felt like doing it. All my life like I wish I can bring up my children like that where you are made to respect it without being scared of anything," he said.

Khan never teaches his children the difference in religion. As a secular person, he teaches them to follow and respect all religions. "I am Muslim. I believe in Islam and I believe it has some really wonderful things...I can teach my son and daughter Islam, the tanets of Islam but I cannot teach them that the other religion is not good enough or better or worse than us. You cannot." He said.

"Sometime, they [his children] ask me what religion they belong to and, like a good Hindi movie hero, I roll my eyes up to the sky and declare philosophically- you are an Indian and your religion is humanity," he said.

Shahrukh Khan just follows the core values of Islam. He is not a specialist of Islam but he truly believes that Islamic scholars are very important for true understanding of Islam. Specialists needs to be there whether it is a religion or any aspect of life. They have to be there to restore the perspective about any religion and they need to explain things in a way, which should be understandable.

Religion can be easily misused. He likes to believe that it is the lack of Education in the large sections of the Islamic world. "I think the youth needs to be educated in world matters, apart from religion. I mean, it's really wonderful to learn your religion. I think it's fantastic for everyone to have a discipline whichever that may be, and respect each other that way, but I think, it's also very important to be educated in worldly affairs. If they do, they will not be misled," he observed.

Explaining the Religion

In 2010, Shahrukh Khan appeared in the movie *My name is Khan*, which is primarily a dramatic love story of an autistic Indian Muslim who marries a Hindu. The movie is about how 9/11 affected the life of this couple without being directly link to it. It also tackles various serious issues, for instance, we must not label people regardless what their creed and nationality is. Lets have peace and tolerance with each other. Let us understand and forgive each other. It tells about the purity, innocence and the goodness of Islam to the rest of the world. It has an Indian emotion that love will conquer everything. It conveys a message that being Muslim is not necessarily being a terrorist. Human beings are a little insecure about each other. They are getting paranoid with each other. That is what dealt in the movie. Do not go by the appearances or religion of other people. Just go by knowing that a good person is a good person and a bad person is a bad person.

Apart from that, one main message of the movie is if two people have a problem on ideological and religious basis, they should communicate with each other. They should explain their religion to each other. They should know well enough how to reply to others to eradicate the misconception about their religion.

Bollywood star Shahrukh Khan is a big believer of the fact that you need to explain your religion to the people who do not understand it. He truly believes that if your religion or region is questioned, explain it. They just need to explain what your discipline stands for. There is a need to accept the fact that there is an issue as far as religion and ideologies are concerned in terms of west, Islam and everywhere. Acceptance of this and explaining will help to sort out the problem in the long run. "If you were to look at it from one side and turn around and say 'listen! You better know my religion.' I think that's not fair. I think we need to....I think not only do they need to explain their religion, they need to understand other religions also and it's a two way process. Just because somebody doesn't understand, of course, they will take it wrongly or react to it wrongly and I think it's a duty of every educated, may be a little liberal Muslim to go out in the world and if he has the opportunity, like I think I have as an actor, I think we need to make sure, that's yes! This is what it stands for, this is what jihad means, this is what tolerance means and this is what Islam means," The actor suggested in an interview with renowned CNN journalist Fareed Zakaria in 2010.

"Whatever little knowledge I have, and I am not fully knowledgeable, and so I find out and try to promote that and tell people. And if you understand it, maybe you will say it – actually no! It's exactly like how our discipline is," He added. If people understand that they will come to realize that all religion including Islam stands for peace, love, kindness and sharing things with each other. It is as beautiful as any other discipline.

It is also written in several verse of holy Qur'an that one of the criteria to go to Jannat(Islamic description of heaven) is to call people toward truth or to explain Islam to others.

Muslims are called the best of people among all the people because they enjoy what is right and forbid what is wrong. The reason almighty God called him best because they convey the message of truth. Therefore, it is the duty of every responsible and conscientious Muslim to convey the message of truth.

According to Shahrukh Khan, it is the duty of every young and educated Muslim to tell people that Islam is one of the most peaceful religion in the world. It is like any other religion. It is about humanity and Goodness. Just because few people have done few wrong things that does not mean everybody is like that. "I like to tell every Muslim that if you don't know your religion well enough, if you are not able to practice it well enough, if your knowledge is less, *Allah tala aapko maaf kar denge*(Allah will forgive you). But, being a Muslim, if you are not able to explain your religion to other people who are not understanding it, *yeh duniya aapko maaf nahi karegi* (the world will not forgive you)," The actor said.

12

Family and Fame

Most of Shahrukh Khan fans love him because he is a well-settled family man. He is at peace with his personal life. His greatest asset is his family. It means more than anything to him. He never brings work at home. He often takes time out of his hectic schedule to spend time with his family.

Shahrukh Khan has mentioned several times that he works hard to bring smiles on people's faces but there are very few people, who are the reason of Shahrukh Khan's smile. His children brings a lot of smile to his face. They are the major source of his sustenance. Khan, who has three children- Aryan, Suhana and Abram, finds spending personal time with them a little more attractive than the whole business of being a star. He starts missing his children when he travels overseas for long duration. His relationship with his children is the most valued relationship. More than anyone else in the world, his children think he is a hero.

The actor loves kids. He is fond of them. He loves spending time with them. He seems so comfortable with them. It is just a natural liking. He feels that it is good for our soul to spend time with children. He has a child-like side. He always wants to impress children with acting. He likes the company of small children. "When I was being trained as an actor, the first thing I thought of was that I should be able to hold the attention of youngsters, little kids because they are the most honest audience that you can get in the world, in every aspect of public appearance," He said. He can spend the whole day in a room full of small children. In fact, he shared his biggest depressions with his children. He does not like to talk to people about his sadness and the only people, he has spoken to, were his beautiful children.

Shahrukh Khan is a regular father. Due to the job that he does, there are some irregularities in the work time but the actor and his family leads a very simple life at home. He has never subjected his children to stardom. The way they are at home is completely separate from the stardom that he has or the image that he creates in films. His children and the rest of the family are not overawed with the fact that he acts in films. They have realized that it is a job that he does.

Shahrukh Khan is not strict. He is just normal with children. He thinks of himself as much younger person because he spends so much time with his children. It makes him so much purer, nicer, gentle and full of life.

His children are very well informed because they travel a lot with him. They have a gift. They have been brought up differently than he was. They have a very different childhood from the childhood that he had. "My parents couldn't afford a lot of things for me but they never made me feel that way. Their parents can afford a lot of things for them but I don't let them feel that way," Shahrukh said.

The actor wants to teach several things to his children. "What I received from my parents is very simple, everyone believes in it: Education is very important. That's something I would pass on to my children. Education is very important but should not become a burden. It should be enjoyable and interesting.

Other than that, my parents taught me that whichever religion you belong to, you should respect it. You should believe in God. There should be something higher than everything else to which you can offer your thanks and from which you can ask for something. Something higher than ever your parents. You can call it any name you want. In my house, we called it *Khuda* or *Allah*. That I would like to pass on to them.

Third, I would like to pass on to them the value of hard work. So if you work hard, educate yourself and respect God, it's a good life. These are simple things, which I think every person knows. My parents too taught me these same things. They may have taught in a different way but these are what I would like to pass on to my kids and I would wish that whichever generation is related to me, the next one will learn from me," the actor mentioned.

As a child, Shahrukh Khan was very attached to his parents. He lost both his parents very early in his life and miss them dearly. Neither of his parents have lived to see his great success in the Hindi film Industry. He prays to them during bad times and misses them in good times. He misses the comfort of being loved unconditionally. He has some great memories of them. When people ask him "why you keep doing what you do," he always gives philosophical answer where he says, "I want to keep on doing it on a bigger screen, so hopefully they [parents] can see it from heaven." He wants to be a huge film star only for them.

As Shahrukh Khan has grown older, he has come to realize that many things that his parents used to tell him did not make sense to him when he was young but he has children now and think about the things that his parents told him. He realized that the things that he did not like doing what his parents told him, he is finding the importance of that when he is having children now. Many things that his parents told him have shaped the person that he is today and made him feel that it is important to look after your family. Good values from his parents and his upbringing played a very crucial role in Shahrukh's life. There is nobody he look up to as his ideals except his parents because they educated him. He spent his childhood with lot of freedom. His family allowed him to grow, as he wanted to. They were very liberal. His parents never stopped him from doing anything but they also taught him how to value things in life. That is the reason why even after reaching such heights there is not a shadow of arrogance in him.

The first hero of Shahrukh Khan is his father Meer Taj Mohammad. He was from Peshawar, British India. Shahrukh had not even passed his childhood times of fun and games when his father died of cancer in 1981. He was just 15 year old then. His father was extremely gentle and soft spoken.

Shahrukh Khan's father had earned his degree in law but he did not make it his career. He chose the business instead. One of the greatest thing, which Shahrukh is very proud of, was that his father fought for India's freedom. He played an active role in the freedom struggle. He was a true patriot. He won a '*tamra-patra*' as a youngest freedom fighter for India. Therefore, Shahrukh Khan feels very responsible, as this country is a gift to him from his father. He has grown up in an atmosphere of having heard many talks of freedom struggle and somehow he feels extremely proud that his father was part of the freedom struggle. Due to this, sometimes he is extremely outspoken when somebody talks about his patriotism or the pride that he takes in being an Indian. He gets disturbed when anyone says wrong about India or raises questions about his patriotism. He gets very emotional when people say that he is not patriotic enough. He finds it very "degrading" and "humiliating" when he has to prove his patriotism. He does not like his patriotism being questioned because he believes that his father fought for the freedom of his country. He feels extremely privileged to have been born in that country. He takes the same amount of pride that anyone takes in his or her own country. His belief in being the secular Citizen of India is so strong that no amount of praise makes him feel extra nice about it and no amount of disrespect makes him think less of his country.

Khan's father Meer Taj Mohammad was an accomplished man and somehow left an impression on his life. Most of the things that he has achieved just because of the teachings of his father. He never thought that his son could be an actor but lot of lines that Shahrukh says in his movies or feelings that he has is because of him. His father taught him some valuable things about life. He always stressed him the importance of being ordinary and working hard. He taught him that it is not special to be special; it is special to be ordinary.

The other thing that Shahrukh's father taught him "The biggest weapon that you have against failure is patience. Not anger, not banging your head against wall, not fate or blaming other people. Just a lot of patience. Though I am very energetic, though I am very jumpy and I do lot of things, which perhaps physically or from the exterior don't seem that I would be a patient person. But, I think, the extreme nature of patience that I have, especially, with my two beautiful, idiotic children and everyone around me in my line of work is because my father taught me that you have to be patient."

Meer Taj Mohammad's values and traditions are still alive and being passed down to Shahrukh Khan's children.

Shahrukh Khan is a believer, utopian, gentle, thoughtful and a little idealistic person like his father but he wants to do all things in life with stomach full of food and have a good car and house. His father was not able to afford many things for him. He used to take him to a roundabout near kamani auditorium in Delhi, where the cars go around. He did not have too much money to buy a film ticket. They could normally afford a packet of peanuts. So, they used to sit in the Centre with peanuts and he would tell Shahrukh "Just these cars passing, if you see it the way I see, it is very enjoyable." They used to watch cars and come home in a bus. Shahrukh Khan thinks that his father was the most successful failure in the world and he is very proud of him. He imbibed the fear of failure that his father go through. He does not want to fail like him. He wants to take his son out and show him movies, not cars around. Therefore, he does not deprecate himself when he says that he is a capitalistic person. It is just that he is a survivor who wants to live well and think well.

Shahrukh Khan's mother Fatima Begum was a magistrate. She was Hyderabadi and very enthusiastic. After his father's death, she dedicated her life to look after both children. She managed those difficult times very well. She managed the responsibility of her kids admirably. She carried on the dream that Shahrukh's father had that their children should be well educated. If they get educated, life will be all right for them. Unfortunately, his mother also failed to stay long enough with him. She died before seeing her son rise to fame and glory.

After his mother died, he left Delhi and moved to Mumbai. He never took any of her possession and things with him. "I didn't take anything. I just felt that if she wanted me to take things that own by her, she would stay here and let me *use* them," He said.

"I just took one television she gave me. It's from Videocon Company. I still remember it and she had bought that for me after I finished my first series in *fauji*. I had bought it with my money but she went with me and bought it for me. That's the only thing I still have," he added.

Downside of Fame

The fear of Shahrukh Khan for his family, especially for his children, is his fame on to them. He always wanted his children not to be affected by the job that he does. He has never made them feel that he is special. The only thing that he wants to do is to make sure that they have a life of their own, which is not under the shadow of tree that he has created through his profession. They should overcome the image of children of a big movie star. This is the only fear that he has in life. He has no other fear. He is confident about the work that he does. He is very grateful for what he has become professionally and what God has given him.

Being a father, he brings a lot of goodness in their life but he feels a little sad that they feel the pressure of his work. "I find them getting a little sensitive about my work. Earlier it wasn't so. I can sense that they can sense that I am sad if things haven't worked out well for me in my work. I still don't bring my work home but I know they can sense it now. I feel they are little down when I am down. I know they feel it's important that their father remain at top. I feel sad at times that they have to feel this pressure of my job. I feel sad." He mentioned. He does not know how to explain many things to them but he can sense that they have pressure that their father should be the biggest star in the world. He tries to give them extra love and protection so they get unaffected by this but he does not think he will be able to avoid this. Therefore, this is perhaps a little sad aspect of his life. In that sense, he thinks they are strong people.

It is true that his name could spoil their lives. He does not want them to ever fight that and say "oh! I am better than my father." He does not want them to become an actor just because he is an actor. They have freedom of choice. He wants them to understand hard work. He believes in good education. He wants to give them best education possible. According to him, they should be educated and hopefully the work that he finish doing by the time, they become old enough to recognize it. It should make them feel a little happy by the job their father do.

13
Philanthropy

Shahrukh Khan, a generous actor, is an active philanthropist. He has been involved in several humanitarian and charity works during his career. He has been associated with several charitable organizations. His image is utilized a lot for public service messages and many other. He freely gives money or other help to people who need it without wanting anything in return. In addition, whenever there is a Campaign being launched, which does some kind of goodness, he promotes it just because of the fact that he is educated and someway it is a good thing for Country, Mankind and Humanity. He has won the UNESCO award for his philanthropic work as well.

Shahrukh Khan believes that he has got more than what he deserves in life and it would be extremely ungrateful if he does not thanks to God and people who are responsible for it. Therefore, he has huge social responsibilities in the position that he has reached and he wants to return to the society.

The actor never prefer to come in limelight for his philanthropic works. He does not make any public display about his social commitments and charity works. He keeps that very private and the reason for keeping that private is his religious beliefs. "Genuinely I am a little Islamic in this. I was brought up with the thought that if you think you are doing a good deed, it's no longer a good deed. Good works, coming from the heart, should be done and forgotten," he explained in a show 'Bollywood Baazigar' in 2006. Every aspect of good work should be done for personal satisfaction of goodness, not for any other reason.

He does not want to capture on camera. He does not want to be talked about. If he believes in a cause, he does it silently. He wants to do it as the essence of life and does not use the persona as an actor to advocate that. "Let me tell you one more thing that I don't feel any pride or happiness or feeling that 'hey, I have done something great today.' I just do it at that point of time because I feel it. I shall be very honest about it. I don't want to say that I feel great helping people. I just do it and I don't want to hear, think, or talk about it," He added.

"Sometimes people would say...'hey this guy is not poor, he is just tricking you for money'. My father used to tell me that if that unfortunate soul had to pretend to be poor and ask for money, that itself is so sad. To be in such a situation is itself an unfortunate thing. So we must help them," he said by adding "To me if somebody at that stage fools me, I find it amusing and I enjoy it. There is a bit of 'illegitimacy' that I like."

He does all through his own funds. He does not like to ask money from others. "I would like to help people with my own private funds rather than, you know, ask for a grant or start a NGO. I think, they are doing a great job but I think it's something that I feel personally, so I should work towards it. I should do a dance on a stage, take that money and help those kids.

In February 2005, Shahrukh Khan performed in the HELP! Telethon Concert with some other Bollywood artists to raise money for the victims of the 2004 Indian Ocean Earthquake.

In October 2008, Shahrukh Khan participated in 'The Rock on for humanity' concert to raise money for helping the children affected by 2008 Bihar flood.

On August 15, 2013, Shahrukh Khan along with other Bollywood personalities took part in a charity show called *Saath hai hum UttaraKhand* raising fund for the Victims of 2013 UttaraKhand tragedy.

In addition to participating in several live programs to raise funds for supporting meaningful causes, Shahrukh Khan actively supports the cause of Education, which is most important in terms of his priorities. He believes that Education is the only key to dismantling hatred, Terrorism and poverty. "It's a very vast thing and I can't do on my own but I would like to help little girls get educate. That is the priority. Poverty can only get eradicated if there is education. It will give chance to stand on their own, look for a job and that's the way. You can't eradicate poverty by, you know, subsidies. I think, Lot of things I have been able to achieve because I was educated finally. Education has helped me a lot. So, I think, Education would be the prime way to remove poverty. *Insha Allah*, in my own small way, if I can do something, I will try my best," he said.

Apart from giving donations and valuable financial help to individuals and foundations, Shahrukh Khan has been involved in numerous philanthropic activities related to Social awareness and health care. For some causes like Cancer or polio, he lends his name because it is important for people to know about the causes of health. As a part of National Rural Health mission of India, he has recorded several public service advertisements regarding good health and child immunization. In that way, it reflects the transfer of an actor's value to a cause.

In the memory of his mother, the actor set up a children's ward at Nanawati Hospital in Mumbai where people suffering from Cancer are treated.

Khan is associated with a number of charitable organization and one such organization is Make a Wish Foundation. He is a member of the board of directors of the foundation in India. This is a non-Profitable organization, originated in United States in 1980, which aims to enrich the lives of Children with Life threatening Medical condition. He has been closely involved with this foundation and has helped them whenever they have approached him.

Khan supports NDTV's Greenathon campaign, an Initiative to make people go Eco-friendly and to provide electricity to various villages in India under the solar energy harnessing project in its title initiative 'Light a Billion lives'. Ever since the Greenathon started, he has been one of the biggest supporter of the Campaign. He has adopted up to twelve villages from 2009 to 2012. His association with such Campaigns has been really rewarding.

Shahrukh Khan's high regard for women is a known fact. He feels strongly about the causes of women. He wants to make public facilities for women in all over India. He dreams of India where women and girls are no longer vulnerable. He dreams of India where people do not have to squat on streets or in bushes. As a goodwill ambassador for WSSCC (Water Supply and Sanitation Collaborative Council), Shahrukh Khan, in 2011, extended the support to water, sanitation and hygiene issues. He joined the effort to improve the quality of life for millions of people in the world. He recorded a public service announcement on the cause in which he said: "Toilets for all will make India cleaner and healthier. Women and girls will be liberated from shame and indignity."

He supports social causes and Campaigns that celebrate and serve women. One such Campaign is MARD or Men Against Rape and discrimination. Indian film actor and director Farhan Akhtar started the Campaign, which works against rape and discrimination of women. In April 2013, Khan got associated with the social campaign in order to raise awareness against rape and discrimination of women. Seen with the moustache, he became the most outstanding face of the Campaign.

In December 2013, Shahrukh Khan was associated with 'Our girls Our Pride'- An initiative taken by NDTV and Vedanta to raise awareness and support for girl child. With Shahrukh Khan participating and appealing to the people about the importance of Campaign, it takes the campaign to a different level of Impact.

14
Awards Rewards and Recognition

Shahrukh Khan, in his illustrious career, has applauded and honored on several platforms for his achievements and contribution to Indian Cinema. Over the years, several awards and recognition have bestowed upon him that have truly recognized his ability as an actor. He also has honors from countries like France and Malaysia where people do not understand Hindi Language.

Shahrukh Khan likes recognizing for his performances. He likes awards. He is like a child when it comes to an award, prize or a present. Whenever he receives an award or honor for his work, he accepts it with graciousness, thankfulness and humility. He feels extremely humble and grateful for all the achievements, awards and distinctions bestowed upon him. He has an immense amount of respect for them. He gets excited with awards. He thinks of awards as something, which gives him huge amount of respect and satisfaction beyond anything else. He likes to believe that awards are the recognition of his work over a period. It gives him a satisfied end to the year. It is a recognition of the work as an actor, star or performer. "I like awards, any kind of award that comes my way. I feel that the entire year's work gets recognized by that one award, whichever it is. So I enjoy the awards. I like the fact that people have liked the work I have done. I love awards. I am greedy about awards. I want all of them," he once quoted. He gets thrilled whatever the level of awards. Sometimes he feels perhaps he does not deserve it but it makes him to work harder. It makes him just to keep on giving a little more what he has given to entertain people.

He attends all the award functions whether he is getting an award or not. He always tries to perform or host them with as much sporting spirit that he has because he truly believes that when all the actors, directors, producers, filmmakers or musicians put their best effort, the only thing they require is applause and that applause reaches to their heart through Award functions.

There is nothing else more thrilling to him than recognized for having done some good works. He has all certificates and medals from his school days. He Keeps them and cherish them. In School, Shahrukh Khan was awarded the 'Sword of honor,' especially the award for best student excelled in sports, studies and extra-curricular activities. He also got Ravi Subramanian Award and Sujit Memorial Award for his outstanding performance in School.

Shahrukh Khan's achievements have been acknowledged at national and international levels. Since 1992, he has won Fourteen Filmfare Awards. He holds the record of receiving maximum numbers of Filmfare Best Actor award, which he shares with Indian Legendary star Dilip Kumar. In addition, He has won many awards in several other Indian film events and award ceremony.

Apart from film Awards; he has been awarded several honors for his contribution to the Indian cinema. In 1997, he was honored with Best Indian Citizen award.

In 2002, he was honored with Rajiv Gandhi Award for "Excellence in the field of Entertainment".

In 2005, the Government of India honored him with the "Padma Shri," a prestigious and India's fourth highest civilian award, for his remarkable contribution towards Indian cinema. Out of the several awards he get, this one looks very much like Shahrukh Khan's best. Interestingly, he has the equivalents of Padma Shri from other countries too.

In 2007, Bollywood Actor Shahrukh Khan was chosen to honor by the French government, with Ordre des arts et des lettres(Order of the Arts and Literature) award for his contribution to Hindi cinema. This was the first time he was honored with such huge International honor. The award is given to people who establish themselves by their creativity in the field of art, culture and Literature or their contribution to the influence of art in France and throughout the world.

Everyone acknowledges that Shahrukh Khan is a great Entertainer. A witness to that is his wax statue at the famous Madame Tussaud wax museum in London, which is a major Tourist attraction. In April 2007, he officially unveiled his wax statue at the museum. Khan's statue is in amidst of great politicians, actors, sportspeople, and leaders of the world. He is extremely proud of that recognition.

In 2008, another wax statue of Shahrukh Khan was installed at famous and prestigious Grevin museum in Paris. He is the only Indian besides Mahatma Gandhi who was honored in such a way. For the actor it is an honor with a great sense of happiness. These wax statues are the reflection of global popularity of Shahrukh Khan.

In 2008, Shahrukh Khan was conferred with the supremely prestigious Malaysian title of "Datuk", which is equivalent to the British knighthood, for promoting tourism in Malacca. A Shahrukh Khan film *One two ka four* (2001) was filmed in Malacca- a tourist destination in Malaysia. He became the first Indian actor to confer with this Prestigious Malaysian title.

In 2008, Shahrukh Khan was recognized among the 50 most powerful people of the world by the prestigious US-based 'Newsweek' magazine. He occupied 41 position in the list and was described as the "King of Bollywood". Events like this prove that Shahrukh Khan is one of the biggest stars of the world.

In July 2009, Shahrukh Khan was awarded with an honorary Doctorate in arts and Culture from Britain's University of Bedfordshire. It has another kind of value because it is a form of recognition from an academic institution. He was nominated for the award by a non-government Organization Routes 2 Roots, which works to bring people and culture together from countries across the subcontinent particularly India and Pakistan. They believed that the best way to bring peace in the world is by people-to-people contact across culture and boundaries. They nominated Shahrukh Khan not only because of his achievements in the Indian film Industry but also because of his charity works.

According to them, he has been working silently for the betterment of the under-privileged children at large. He has been pro-active whenever the need arises for natural calamities. Khan accepted the award with great pride and said that he aimed to use the award to help underprivileged children who does not get the opportunity to educate themselves.

In 2010, Shahrukh Khan, along with his frequent onscreen partner Kajol was invited to officially ring the opening bell at NASDAQ, the world's biggest stock exchange, in New York as a part of promotion of *My name is Khan*. This was the first time that Indian stars were invited to ring the bell at NASDAQ.

In 2011, Khan was honored with the UNESCO's *Pyramid con Marni* award at the 20th UNESCO awards held in Germany for his charity works and charitable commitment towards providing education for children, becoming the first Indian who was honored with such huge respect."I promise myself and I promise you that I will extend the goodness, the education and the well-being that I want from my children to the rest of the children and the rest of the world," He said at the award ceremony. By winning this international award, he set an example of not just being an actor but also a leader in Philanthropy.

In April 2012, Yale University presented Shahrukh Khan with its Chubb Fellow award, its most prestigious award for Leadership. He became the first Bollywood personality who was honored with such notable honor.

Adding to his growing list of notable achievements, Shahrukh Khan received the prestigious brand-laureate legendary award by Asia-Pacific brands foundation in 2012 for his outstanding Contribution to the Hindi Film Industry.

In 2012, the International Film Festival in Marrakech paid tribute to Shahrukh Khan. He was conferred with Morocco's prestigious Medal of honor. His movies was shown with subtitles at the festival.

Shahrukh Khan has been featured regularly in the listing of the most powerful names of Hindi cinema. In January 2013, he created history by becoming the first Indian actor to feature on the cover of Forbes India Magazine, a feat unparalleled in the Indian film Industry. The Magazine described him as "Shah Rukh

Inc. - India's biggest brand" and named him the most powerful celebrity of India's media and entertainment sector. He was ranked at number one among India's most powerful Entertainment icons. The ranking was based on income and popularity of India's biggest entertainers across eight categories: Film actors, directors, sport stars, TV personalities, Singers/Musicians, authors, models and comedians. In 2014, he retained the same spot in the second edition of Forbes India's Celebrity 100 list.

In December 2013, NDTV included Khan amongst the India's 25 greatest Global Living Legends of all time and President Mr. Pranab Mukherjee honored him for his invaluable Contribution towards Indian Cinema.

In 2014, Khan was appointed as Goodwill Ambassador for Korea to promote goodwill and mutual understanding between the people of two countries.

In May 2014, Bollywood actor Shahrukh Khan emerged as the second wealthiest actor on a Wealth-X Hollywood and Bollywood Rich list with an estimated personal fortune of USD 600 Million. American Comedian Jerry Seinfeld topped the list with an estimated net worth of USD 820 million. Wealth-X is the world's Leading ultra high net worth (UHNW) intelligence and prospecting firm.

Wealth-X said, "Khan is estimated to be worth $600 million. Immensely popular around the globe as well as in his home country, India, Khan is also a Producer, TV host, co-owner of an Indian cricket club and a philanthropist. He has appeared in more than 50 Bollywood films and is a regular at the annual Cannes Film Festival."

Khan was the only Bollywood star in the list. He was placed above biggest stars of Hollywood. The actor commented on the list in an interview of Hindustan Times by saying that: "I do feel happy, but these are just names given to somebody who is doing something that people feel is special. These are standard measures. They don't define you."

"I think I am rich because I have beautiful children," he added.

In July 2014, Shahrukh Khan was conferred with France's highest civilian honor- Knight of the Legion of Honor- a recognition for his contribution to cultural diversity across the world. He was extremely humbled and grateful by the distinction conferred upon him."It would be wrong for me to accept it as an individual so I accept it on the behalf of hundreds and thousands of Indian Filmmakers who have worked tirelessly," He told after accepting the honor.

In October 2014, Shahrukh Khan has been presented the Global Diversity award at the Britain's House of Commons in London for his outstanding contribution to Global Diversity.

In April 2015, Shahrukh Khan received the award for outstanding achievement in Cinema at the fifth annual - The Asian Awards. He was very "grateful" and "humbled" by this honor.

In October 2015, the University of Edinburgh, where Shahrukh Khan was invited to deliver a speech to their students, awarded him with an honorary doctorate. He received the doctorate on the behalf of all the people who have been behind his success and recognition. "An honor like this is least expected and it makes you think back upon the journey that you had and got you to the place where you are and you realize that there is a great pride in the work I have done and at the same time you realize it is not an individual endeavor at all. It is actually because of hundreds of people putting huge amount of hard work into making me who I am," he said.

Being a star

Shahrukh Khan is a magnanimous actor whose quick rise to superstardom is an inspirational story for young people. He is an actor who becomes a big star. He has certain star qualities and charisma that makes him ultimately the star that he is. That is why he is so popular. He is widely known in different parts of the world. He gets pleasantly surprise when people recognize him in countries like France and Germany, as the language of Indian films is very different from them. Few movie stars enjoy the fame and recognition that Shahrukh Khan does. He enjoys the fact that people gives him so much love and appreciation. Every little bit of attention that he gets; he finds it little less. He wants more. He loves the fact that people scream when he enters in a film's frame. He enjoys every bit of it. He believes that you get this opportunity only once in a lifetime or maybe not. He has given that opportunity and he wants to grab it.

He is immensely proud that he has no privacy in public places. He has never complained about lack of privacy or rescheduling of his life according to the films or work that he does. He finds it very stupid when he sees stars wearing dark glasses to hide their faces. He loves the fact that he does not wear dark glasses. In his words, "All my life I worked towards to be recognized. I don't want to spend my life now hiding my face. I love people's smile. They look at me; they wave up to me. I enjoy all. I am immensely proud that I have no privacy and what's the point if I am a star and nobody knows me." He wants to be known. He wants to be troubled and disturbed for as many years possible. He lives for people to follow him. It does not really bother him.

The biggest thing that Shahrukh Khan has is the fact that people know him and love him as their own. He enjoys being in the public eye. "I enjoy my stardom. I would give my left hand and right hand to live this life all over again," he quoted once. He loves his stardom. He is very easy and casual about it. He generally wears his stardom like a T-shirt. He does not wear it like a Tuxedo.

Leading a star's life is something that he always wanted. He feels nice to be a movie star. He truly believes that he was born to be a star. He does not need an occasion to be a star. He loves being a star. It is the greatest moment of his everyday life when people smile by seeing him on road. When people come to greet him, he entertains them and makes them happy. He likes all the trappings of glamour and success. He does not want to lead a private life in public places. He is unabashedly happy being so well known.

People generally ask him don't you like walking on the roads and having *Dahi-vada* on *chaupati*? Do you want to be just a normal person? Don't you want to do normal things in life? The answer is simply No. He does not want to walk on the roads. He likes to fly in a private jet. He does not want to have a normal life. He is very happy being a star. He would miss being a star too much if he would be a normal person.

He loves being recognized. He would not be able to walk on the road if people did not mob him. He does not want that recognition to go away because he lives for it. When large number of people loves an actor, when so many screams happens, they start believing somewhere that they are special. Nothing can happen. No one can take that recognition away from him or her. It is a defense mechanism that comes into a celebrity's life. It keeps them alive. It keeps them going. The actor believes that one of the most unfortunate things of being a star is that they start believing their immortal in a good way.

Shahrukh Khan believes that the only quest that human being have is the quest for permanence and that recognition is never going to be permanent. He knows that it will go one day in some part of his life. However, he does not think about losing that recognition. He believes that if he starts thinking about it, he will be losing out what he is getting right now.

He is fearless and has nothing to lose. He does things, which he feels like doing. He came to Mumbai with nothing but dreams. He was nobody. He believes that how much ever you take away from him, you cannot deny the fact that there was a time in Mumbai when he was the ultimate king of Hindi film Industry and people really liked him. "I have gained so much. I have got so much that if you took away everything from me, you still not be able to take away the 73 films that I have done," he said. In India, people feel him. He is not just a name; he is a feeling, which people cannot deny. Therefore, if he is a feeling, then he has nothing to lose.

Printed in the United States
By Bookmasters